House of

Testo

sterone

Sharon O'Donnell

10-digit ISBN: 0-9778086-0-2
13-digit ISBN: 978-0-9778086-0-1
Library of Congress Control Number: 2006937389

Editing by Henry Oehmig and Arlene Prunkl
Book Design by Fiona Raven
Cover Illustration by Josué Menjivar

First Printing 2007
Printed in Canada

Published by Jefferson Press

j e f f e r s o n   p r e s s
P.O. Box 115
Lookout Mountain, TN 37350

20.00

For my boys . . .

Contents

Introducing
the Lady of the House

THIS IS A book for all those mothers and wives out there who live in a constant quandary of figuring out the sons and husbands in their lives. It's especially for those moms who are outnumbered by males in their own household and find themselves struggling to retain their identity as a woman and their sanity as a human being. There is so much testosterone bouncing around my own male-dominated home that if you were to walk through our door, you would risk growing a testicle. Our home is filled with bathroom jokes, roughhousing, televised sports (or *Power Rangers*), and miscommunication. Forget those reality survival shows set in the jungle or on remote islands; the real question is how does the lady of the house survive?

I'm with you. I feel your pain. As the only female in a house I share with my husband and three sons, I'm continually challenged in my everyday life as Mars and Venus collide head on. Simple living was difficult enough when it had been just my husband, Kevin, and myself; even then I sometimes had trouble communicating with him and became distinctly aware of the differences in the thinking processes of men and women. Then, in 1991, after three years of marriage, son No. 1, Billy, arrived, and the odds were instantly stacked against me. With the birth of David, our second son, in 1994, I knew our household was destined to be controlled by the male hormone and that my world would never be quite the same again. My young boys grew up calling me "The Female," compliments of their dad. It wasn't an ideal situation, but I was gradually becoming accustomed to it.

Then, in 2000, along came Jason, son No. 3, the little brother with a big attitude. The odds shot up to four to one in their favor. By that time, nobody, including myself, was going to place any bets on me keeping my sanity. And add to this lopsided ratio Fenway, our long-haired Dachshund, whom we brought into the family in 2004. He was named after the home of the Boston Red Sox—Fenway Park. (Kevin and the boys are huge Red Sox admirers, since Kevin's family is from that area.) Call me difficult to please, but even a girl dog would make the situation in our house a bit more pleasant; they're quicker to train, and you wouldn't have to worry about girl dogs "bothering" Jason's stuffed animals, if you know what I mean.

So it's no coincidence that the first part of the word *testosterone* begins with the word *test*. My guys continue to put me to the test every day, and I'm starting to realize males and females are simply not meant to live together. I suspect there was something in the Bible centuries ago about that. Originally, there were eleven commandments—"Thou shalt not live together, male and female, in the same dwelling for chaos and confusion shalt result"—but somehow it got deleted along the way. Probably Moses, Paul, Mark, and the other fellows realized they would need some way to get hot meals and someone to watch the kids, so they opted to take literary license with God's words. Just my theory.

Whenever a marketer calls and asks for "the lady of the house," I have to pause a second before I respond. That title annoys me because it's such a misnomer. It sounds so regal, so respected, as if everyone else in the house puts mom on a pedestal. Nothing could be further from the truth. We might be referred to as the "lady of the house" during a telephone call from a salesperson, but as soon as the call is over, we go back to our tasks like cleaning the toilets with super-strength Pine-Sol, hoping in vain that the guys have taken better aim at the toilet this week.

Since 1998, I've written a family life column for *The Cary News*, a community newspaper in Cary, North Carolina. Many of my columns have dealt with the situation of being the only female in a houseful of males, and I found that this particular subject received more response than did columns concerning other matters. Sympathetic women from the area responded with unexpected support and humor. I soon realized that women like myself were surviving in houses of testosterone all over the country—even the world—and that it was my duty to reach out to them. Thus, the idea for this book was born. What you will find between these covers is a collection of new essays based on my columns about the experience of being a woman outnumbered in her own home.

To further help all of you distressed ladies of the house, I have also developed a website called *www.momsofboys.org*, which includes many informational links about raising sons, lists of suggested reading for parents of boys and boys themselves, movie suggestions for moms and sons, advice from other moms, a message board to post questions, a Moms of Boys (MOB) Club page where moms can start or join a local group, a sampling of my humor columns, and much more.

Once I had made up my mind to write this book, the first and most important step I faced was choosing an appropriate title. This idea sprang quite naturally from a real event in my life. Kevin and I were attending a dinner and play with a medieval theme, which was a rare evening out for us (one of our nieces was in the play, so Kevin was obligated to go). Part of the fun included announcing each couple as they arrived, and we were asked to quickly invent a medieval title for the two of us, much to my creatively challenged husband's chagrin. "That's easy," I assured him as I leaned over to whisper a title to the dinner's organizer. When we were introduced by a young lady with an English accent as "The King and Queen of the House of Testosterone," there were a lot of knowing laughs in the audience of diners. Everyone either knows first-hand or suspects what an excess of powerful testosterone can do to a home.

Exhibit A: my home. This book is a glimpse into my life as the only lady of the house—a closeup look at the mayhem of marriage and motherhood to which all wives and mothers can relate, particularly those with sons. Perhaps by sharing my domestic, maternal, and marital dilemmas with others, I can survive, and so can you. Or at least we can have a laugh while we hang on by the thinnest of threads.

1

A Son is Given unto Our House (ditto…ditto again)

— Sure Signs You're the Mother of Boys —

+ You automatically wipe off the toilet seat before you sit down.

+ Your weekend schedule includes more total hours of little league sports than it does sleep.

+ The lamp in your family room is held together by Super Glue in three places.

+ You can carry on a conversation about athletic cup sizes with the college-aged guy at the sporting goods store with no blushing or embarrassment whatsoever.

+ The hospital ER staff offered your family a "Frequent User" card.

+ The Sunday suit you bought your son six months ago is hanging in his closet with the price tags still dangling. And he's already outgrown it.

+ You have to arrange two weeks ahead of time to take a bubble bath—and then must lock the door and scream, "I'm in the tub—ask Dad!" every three minutes.

+ You can get your sons to eat broccoli just by telling them whoever eats the most, wins.

◆ The Third Child

In the beginning, there was just a man named Kevin and a woman named Sharon living in the House of O'Donnell, and both enjoyed equal rule in this house. Then came the blessings of two sons, turning our reasonably tranquil abode into a veritable House of Testosterone, quickly known throughout the land (or at least the neighborhood) as a place of pandemonium. I don't recall officially abdicating my throne, but I was definitely losing power in my household. And then came son number three.

When I found out I was pregnant with our third child, I told my husband, Kevin, the news via e-mail. Yeah, you're damn right I was chicken. We'd been debating whether or not we should try for a third one. Since my biological clock was ticking, I was for it, while he was hesitant, viewing a baby as just one more college education to save for. To have or not to have, that was the question. Whenever we talked about the issue, Kevin rolled his eyes like one of those Vegas slot machines, but instead of fruits scrolling up in the windows, I could tell he was looking at dollar signs: $$$$$. This made it difficult to reason with him about the advantages of having another child.

I figured with an e-mail I could at least get in all I wanted to say before he started screaming or passed out. He'd be sitting there at his desk, and—*bam!*—suddenly, there it would be in bold type, amid all those other e-mails from clients. This way he'd have ample time to think about how to respond to the news. Maybe he'd even rush home with roses in his arms (ha!).

The "whether to have a third child" question had first popped up in our home about three years earlier when our two sons, Billy and David, were six and three. Since we had two boys, it was only natural for me to daydream about having a little girl, but another boy would be all right with me, too, even though the thought of having to keep up with boys' hand-me-down clothes for the next decade made me feel slightly nauseated. One night as we were cleaning up the kitchen before bedtime, I finally got up the nerve to ask Kevin, "What do you think about having another one?"

He paused a second, then looked at me and shrugged his shoulders. "But where would we sit in restaurants?" he asked. I waited for him to finish his thought, but then I realized he actually was finished. That was the entire thought. I tried— I *really* tried—to figure out what in the heck he was talking about, but finally I had to ask what he meant. "All the tables and booths and stuff are for families of four," Kevin explained. "If we have another child, how would we all sit down in a restaurant together?"

I froze in the middle of loading the dishwasher, the absurdity of his response paralyzing me for a few moments. Even if this imaginative but dumb reason had appeared in some physician's top-ten list of why not to have kids, it didn't apply to us because we hardly ever went out to eat unless I begged or hinted that TV dinners were the only food left in the house. Then, deciding to play his game, I offered, "Well, I guess we could always opt for the drive-thru." Oddly, this seemed to appease Kevin, and he nodded thoughtfully, perhaps mentally calculating the cost of a lifetime of Happy Meals.

I dropped the topic for that day, sensing he was not in the right mind frame for such a serious discussion. He knew that I wanted another baby, but he also knew as time went by and we got further away from the diaper bag routine, the harder it would be to start over with the sleepless nights, the potty training, and the loss of free time.

Yet there was this part of me that just didn't want to accept the idea that I'd never hold another one of my babies in my arms, feel it flutter inside me for the first time, hear another first laugh. I wanted to experience those magic years again.

And certainly, part of me really wanted to have a girl. Let's face it—the odds were stacked against me every day of my life. Three guys versus me. I had just about reached the point of waving the white flag, but I was still hanging in there. A little girl would be nice, but I admit I was much more adept at handling ball practices than ballet lessons. I was pretty good at jump shots but awful at standing on my tiptoes and twirling around. I had no idea how to tie a bow in someone's hair, yet I could wet down cowlicks and shave sideburns. I'd have to learn how to be a mother to a daughter, but I was willing to try. It became my dream to have another female in the house.

Just once, I wanted to buy a Barbie instead of a Power Ranger or GI Joe. Or one of those pink castles with the princess in the window or the little refrigerator with the plastic vegetables. However, my husband's main objection to having another baby was to make sure there was plenty of college money set aside for each child. Admirable, but just too darn much like the financial analyst he is. We'd done a good job with saving for our first two, but we would have to start over saving for our third. No doubt it would have been easier to stop at two. But my own parents had "started over" when they decided to have me, their fourth child, when their youngest at the time was eight years old. If they'd decided differently...would I have never been born? Sure, I knew having another one wouldn't be easy, but it was going to be worth it.

We also had a few living-space issues we'd have to work out if we had a third baby; the playroom would need to be converted into a bedroom, and all the junk in there needed to be relocated.

There were other times when the problem of having enough space in the house entered my mind. Once, when we had a tornado warning, I rushed the boys into our small downstairs bathroom in the center of the house, which experts say is the safest place in this situation. As the three of us sat there with pillows piled around us, crammed into the tiny area, I wasn't thinking about the weather. I was mulling over ways to fit a third child in there during such emergencies. I had begun looking at every event in our lives from this third-child perspective.

Then there was the proverbial "the clock is ticking" problem. When we started talking abut the possibility of a third one, I was thirty-six and still had time, I thought, but I didn't want to wind up on the cover of *The National Enquirer* with the headline, "Sixty-Year-Old Gives Birth to Triplets!" That same year, when I went in for my annual gynecological exam, I had to see the new doctor, a man in his late twenties, who also happened to be very attractive, which can be rather embarrassing in that situation. I sat in a chair as he looked over my chart. Then he turned to me and said, "Soooo…I guess your child-bearing years are over." He posed it partly as a question and partly as an indisputable fact. I had a powerful urge to reply, "Yep, that's right. Just put me out to pasture with Old Nellie. We're off to the glue factory now." I swear I could feel my ovaries drying up as I sat in his office chair, my eggs being zapped by a microscopic laser gun with a neon light flashing "Game Over!"

Instead, I smiled at his absence of tact and answered, "I'm not sure if we're done—probably, I guess." I was wallowing in indecisiveness. Inside, I was in turmoil as images of Billy and David as babies swirled through my mind. I kept thinking, no more watching the first steps, hearing the words *ma-ma* for the first time. Something inside me was aching, empty, and this was the moment that Kevin now refers to as "the decision-maker." He often says it was the doctor's comment about my childbearing days being over that made me decide what I wanted for sure.

He might be right. Honest to God, I felt like such an old has-been mare when I left that doctor's office that I almost neighed. I was determined to prove to that doctor it was too early to write me off in the baby-making department. I could envision him putting a check mark on my chart in the box labeled, "Done having kids." I wanted to remind him of the Bible story about Abraham and Sarah, who was, like, a hundred years old when she had a baby, and that was before *in vitro* fertilization.

Kevin considered suing the doc for prompting me to lean toward having a baby, but he couldn't come up with anything that would stick in court. "Maybe if he could be made to pay the kid's tuition," Kevin would wonder aloud. Money again.

Still, our indecision about this as a couple was frustrating. There were times at our house when things got incredibly hectic and noisy, such as when David was four and his infamous temper flared up while seven-year-old Billy squirted glue on the carpet as he worked on a school project that was due the next day. Amid the chaos and the screams, Kevin would joke and imitate my voice, saying, "I want a third one!"

One time, after another similar incident, I looked at Kevin and said, "You don't understand how I feel. You can have a baby when you're seventy if you want to. I can't."

He jerked his head toward me, his eyes wide. "I don't want to have a baby when I'm seventy!" he bellowed.

"Yeah," I pouted, "but the point is you could if you wanted to. Nature's not fair."

Just to be on the safe side, I started taking vitamins containing folic acid because I knew it played a vital role in reducing birth defects. When Kevin was ready, I wanted to be ready. And so the discussion went back and forth for over a year until one glorious day when another couple we knew who'd also been contemplating the "third-child question" told me they were expecting a baby. This, I knew, was major ammunition for my cause. As soon as I told him about our friends' impending blessed event, I saw the look of resignation in Kevin's eyes. It was time to go and buy the latest baby names book.

I became pregnant on the first try, just like I'd done with the other two (let me just say to that doctor who thought my childbearing years were behind me—*na-na, na, na-na!*). I was pretty sure by the way my body was feeling that the deed was done, but I kept my suspicions to myself. Kevin, of course, lost all track of the days on the calendar and didn't have a clue. Finally, I took a pregnancy test, and as I watched the plus sign gradually appear before my eyes, my heart started beating really fast. I dropped to my knees beside the bathtub and cried from sheer happiness, praying to God to please be with me as I carried this child and for the baby to be healthy. And to please minimize the stretch marks.

Then I sat down and typed the e-mail. I punched "Send" and waited. About thirty minutes later, I heard the garage door go up, signaling Kevin's early arrival home from work. When he came around the corner into the study where I was, his face was pale. Beyond pale actually. I put my fingers on his wrist to make sure he had a pulse. His chin quivered a little as he said, "I got your e-mail." Then he reached out and hugged me, though I heard him mutter under his breath, "I'm gonna kill that damn doctor."

✦ THREE OF A KIND

AT LAST THE TIME had come to tell the boys they were going to have a new sibling. (Insert music from *Jaws* here). No one knew whether it would be a sister or a brother, but it would definitely mean changes in our household. As we walked into Cici's Pizza, I gave Kevin a knowing smile and nodded toward Billy and David, who were oblivious to how important this night would be. I was so excited I was about to burst, although I was nervous, too. I wasn't sure how they'd react, but I couldn't imagine them being anything but deliriously happy—like their mother. Do all pregnant women turn pathetically naïve, or was it just me?

Billy, eight, and David, five, chomped away at their pepperoni and cheese pizza, and before I could think of a proper plan of attack, they were done eating and were pleading for quarters for those obnoxious video games. We relented since it was a special night. "We'll tell them during dessert," I whispered to Kevin. While they went off together, the two of us devised a scheme.

"I'll talk first," I said, knowing there were a few things I'd want to say before we broke the news. "I'll tell them how much we love them and how it has made us want to add to our family and share that love."

"Give me a break," Kevin replied, sticking his finger into his mouth and pretending to gag himself.

"Too sentimental?" I asked.

"They're guys. They don't need to hear that stuff."

"Okay, then," I said. "You start." He nodded and took a bite of cheese bread, seemingly unmoved by the importance of the moment. "What're you going to say?" I prodded.

"I'll handle it," he told me with a "don't worry about it" wave of his hand. That remark scared me a bit, but since this baby had been mostly my desire, I was just glad he wanted to take an active part in telling the boys.

When they came back, I got them plates of their favorite gooey chocolate dessert slices. They started shoveling spoonfuls into their mouths, and I glanced over at Kevin. He bit into a cinnamon bun and stared at the big screen TV, so I kicked him under the table—gently, of course, or at least that was my intent. He sighed, wiped his mouth with a napkin and cleared his throat. "Guys," he began. (At the same time I silently cursed because I'd forgotten to bring a camera to capture this moment in our family history.) "I have something to tell you." They both looked over at him, intrigued, chocolate dripping from their mouths, their eyes sparkling.

Kevin took a deep breath and said point blank, "Someone is

coming to live with us." I turned to him, perplexed, wondering from which parenting book he'd gotten this gem of wisdom.

David asked gleefully, "Grandma? Is it Grandma?"

"No, it's not Grandma, thank God," Kevin said. I wasn't sure if he was talking about his mother or mine, so I let that one slide. Besides, I doubted either of the grandmas would want to live in our testosterone-dominated household. They had their own lives still intact. A silent prayer of "Dear God, let it be a girl this time," slipped from my thoughts before I could stop it, but I followed that with a quick, "I didn't mean that, God. Just let it be healthy and make sure my epidural works."

"How 'bout Jeff?" David asked, referring to a neighbor boy who played over at our house quite frequently. "Is it Jeff?" Now our big moment was veering way off course. I smacked Kevin on the shoulder of his leather jacket like I was swatting a fly.

"No, it's not Jeff," I said, feeling like we were slipping into a game of Twenty Questions.

Billy swallowed a mouthful of dessert and blurted, "It's a baby, isn't it?"

I smiled. Here was my chance to have a Kodak moment with my son, a chance to make a memory we'd cherish forever. "Yes, Billy," I said, "we're going to have a baby." Then I noticed the panicked expression on his face and his huge, frightened blue eyes. To my surprise, tears began to trickle down his cheeks. My mouth dropped open. "Bill, what's the matter, sweetheart?"

"I don't want a baby," he said between sobs. "I like things the way they are now!" Then he jumped up and ran into the restroom. This, of course, was not the jubilant reaction I'd envisioned.

"Uh, do we have a plan B?" asked Kevin.

I looked at my beloved, way beyond perturbed. "Go get him, Kev."

Kevin leaned over and patted me on the shoulder. "Just give him a minute. He'll be okay."

"I can't believe this," I said, slouching in the seat. I noticed David was giving me a snaggly-toothed grin. "How ya doing, buddy?" I asked.

"Good," he replied. This is still his stock answer to almost every question; David's always been a boy of few words. I eyed the men's room door, but Billy still wasn't making his exit.

I turned to David again. "You do realize I'm going to have a baby, right?" He nodded while checking out the cartoon on the overhead TV. "How do you feel about that?" I asked, sounding like a psychologist charging by the hour.

"Good."

I gave up trying to have a sentimental moment with David and decided to count my blessings that he wasn't having a meltdown like Billy. I gazed at the bathroom door again and sighed.

"Okay," Kevin said, "I'm going, I'm going." He went into the restroom and found Billy there, still crying. He was able to get Billy back out into the restaurant, but we left immediately. I certainly had no more appetite. As I we got into the car, I saw Kevin's red-rimmed eyes and realized he'd been crying in the bathroom, too. I was touched by his sensitivity to his son's feelings, but it still kind of vexed me that they had conducted their own psychotherapy session in a bathroom stall. I mean, come on, guys, I was the one who would be gaining thirty pounds here.

The drive home was quiet. Billy stared out the window. I knew he was hurt and angry. He wasn't a child who dealt well with change, and I should have remembered that. After all, he was the one who once begged us not to sell our old car because it was his "buddy." He was a status quo kid. David, on the other hand, didn't seem to be affected one way or the other by the news as he sat happily licking his after-dinner lollipop.

A few hours after we got home, Billy finally calmed down. I took a risk and brought out photo albums of the boys' baby pictures. I was relieved when Billy started leafing through them, even smiling as he pointed to some of them. By the end of the night, Billy admitted, "I guess it would be kind of neat to have a baby." But I could tell he wasn't truly convinced, that he was saying it for my benefit.

Weeks later, he told me he had been afraid that if I had a baby, I wouldn't do things with him any more. After swallowing the lump in my throat, I assured him that I would always have time for him, that we'd still have fun together, too. Thank goodness, over the next few months, Billy became genuinely excited about his new sibling and started calling it "our baby." I loved hearing those words because this meant he had finally accepted the pregnancy and was looking forward to having a new brother or sister.

I made sure to have plenty of bonding time with Billy and David to make it an event we would all gladly anticipate. Sometimes they'd both sit next to me with their hands on my stomach, waiting to feel the small movements of the baby. What an amazing feeling that is and how blessed I felt to share that with my sons. Kevin and the boys went with me to some of my appointments, so Billy and David could take part in hearing the whooshing sound of the baby's heartbeat, a sound that had captivated Kevin and me when we first heard it during my pregnancy with Billy.

A few months passed, and the early ultrasounds showed that the baby seemed to be healthy, which is always an enormous relief. Doctors asked Kevin and me at an ultrasound appointment if we wanted to know the sex of the baby. We both did. I wanted to find out, so I could decorate the room accordingly, buy new clothes, throw out or keep the boys' hand-me-downs, and mostly to prepare myself. More than anything, I wanted a third child, but if given an option, I have to admit I would have placed an order for a girl.

My older sister, Gail, also has three boys, although there is an age difference between them and my sons. Her youngest is a year older than Billy, and the two of them would pal around quite often when they were kids. Gail's family lived nearby, and so I'd had a front-row seat during my nephews' growing-up years. I'd seen the bedlam that occurred in a household with three boys. To be honest, during my early years of marriage, I was sometimes left in shock after observing her boys, their roughhousing and sibling arguments. I'd think to myself, "My kids will never be that loud, and they will never think farting is funny." Yep, the joke's on me.

So I'd seen what was at stake with the gender of this third child. And if we ended up having another boy, I didn't want to find out first in the delivery room and let even the tiniest bit of disappointment mar the joy of his birth.

Problem was, the baby had situated itself so as to hide its private parts. Ah, modesty. It must be a girl. Because of my "advanced" age of thirty-eight years and to prevent any possible complications in utero, we were scheduled for a more detailed ultrasound and amniocentesis at a nearby hospital. This time the baby was in a position that revealed its gender, so the nurse, who knew we had two boys already, asked if we were prepared to know the sex. We nodded.

She pointed a laser light to the area in question and said, "Three of a kind. It's another boy." I smiled and then chuckled as my eyes met Kevin's. Another boy seemed to be in the cards for us. Three of a kind, indeed. Still, this was followed by a slight twinge of disappointment—disappointment that I'd never buy Barbies or lacy dresses, that I'd never hear her giggle with friends about which boys they thought were cute, that I'd never plan a wedding with my daughter.

Kevin knew how I felt and patted my shoulder. "Three boys, Boss," he said, calling me the nickname he'd given me years earlier. "We've had a lot of fun with the first two, haven't we?"

"Yeah," I mumbled. "We have." I smiled at Kevin's efforts to make sure I was feeling okay.

"Well, here we go again," Kevin remarked. He looked genuinely happy. And I was honestly looking forward to every little boy bit of it.

Still, as we walked outside, I fumbled for my cell phone in my purse. I felt the sudden need to talk to my mother. "Everything's fine with the baby," I told her, and she sighed in relief. "But, Mama, it's another boy." Tears quickly pooled in my eyes as I realized how much I'd wanted to have the kind of relationship with a daughter of my own that my mother and I shared.

"That's all right, that's fine," she said. "You know, that little boy is going to be so precious. I can't wait to hold him." Somehow just hearing her voice tell me that made me feel better, and the tears forming in my eyes disappeared. My disappointment vanished, replaced by thankfulness that the baby was healthy and thriving. I'd gladly take another boy. After all, he was "our baby."

✦ Getting Ready

When I see pregnant women who look like they could burst at any minute, it takes me back to those uncomfortable yet exciting days in my own life. Billy had felt like he'd been trying out for the U.S. gymnastics team inside of me, doing flips and somersaults every half hour (is it any wonder he was born with the umbilical cord wrapped around his neck twice and tied in a knot?), and David and Jason both seemed to be practicing Tai Kwon Do in the womb, a foot or knee always jabbing me in the side. Trying to sleep was almost impossible and snacking on Tums got old very quickly.

In the days of late pregnancy when I was waiting for Jason to be born, I started worrying because I hadn't yet bought the required school supplies for my other sons, who were about to start a new school year. If I went into labor without buying the supplies, Kevin would *never* get the right notebooks, pencils, and folders required on those very specific school supply lists. It's funny how women dwell on such small things when faced with much bigger issues.

But this was also a time when I could hardly contain my excitement about the baby boy inside me. I couldn't wait to finally see the little guy. I wondered how he would resemble his brothers or my husband and me. I daydreamed of holding him, listening to his first cries, and readied myself for smelling like spit-up and Preparation H for the next few months of my life.

Kevin, the boys, and I had a lot of fun preparing for Jason's impending birth. Kevin bought a little onesie outfit for the baby to wear home from the hospital, and on the front was a picture of Billy and David with the caption, "My Big Brothers." Sometimes even Kevin can be sentimental. Of course, he also bought me a T-shirt with "Honorary Member of the O'Donnell Male Club" printed on it, so he wasn't exactly going to turn soft on me anytime soon.

Billy and David also made preparations for the baby's arrival. The old playroom had to be converted into Billy's room, while Billy's old room became David's and David's bedroom became the baby nursery. Too bad those TV home makeover shows weren't around back then because we could have used some help. The boys undertook the arduous job of switching toys from room to room, while I had to sort through and box up hand-me-downs, a task so awful that it makes having a pap smear seem appealing.

We'd also been trying to decide on a name for the baby, rambling through those baby books that list the meaning and origin of names. Finally, we all decided on the name "Jason," though I'm not sure why. Kevin and I liked it, and the boys did, too—one of the few names we actually agreed upon. I suspect the reason Billy and David preferred it was that the red Power Ranger was named Jason—a good enough reason for me at that stage of the game. The middle name would be either Steven or Thomas, named in honor of Kevin's grandfather, but we managed to procrastinate making that final call.

We had named Billy after Kevin's father, William Robert

O'Donnell, who died in 1986 in his fifties. With our second son, "David" happened to be one of my favorite guy names, although Kevin claims it was because I dated a guy in college named David whom I really liked. Truth is, I dated about six or seven guys named David, and one of the reasons I dated them was that their name sounded so nice to me.

I wanted David's middle name to be my maiden name, Johnson, and at the time I was blissfully unaware of the more risqué meanings concerning the male anatomy that were associated with this moniker. I'd walked around for twenty-five years of my life as Sharon Johnson, and not once did I hear about this other meaning until after David was born, and I read something in a newspaper column about "Johnson" being a slang term. How could they do that to such a fine, time-honored name? Even if I had known the "alternative" meaning of my family's name, we still would have chosen it for David anyway, but it was a strange and perplexing thing to find out at the time I did.

Now of course, T-shirts with the "Johnson" phrases are everywhere. I can just imagine a time when David is older, and he and the guys in the college dorm room are trading, shall we say, fish stories about sizes of certain parts of the anatomy. I can picture David boasting with a cowboy swagger and narrowed eyes, "Hey, buddy, my middle name is Johnson."

Another preparation thing we did was to take the boys to a class for big brothers at the local hospital. This type of class lets the children see what it's like to have a baby around the house and what it means to be the older sibling. To my surprise, Billy was highly enthusiastic about learning more about babies, despite his outburst when he first learned I was pregnant. Since

his initial reaction, he'd done a complete turnaround and was
ecstatic about the impending birth. David still seemed to be
rather unemotional about the whole thing, concentrating more
on his Nintendo Game Boy than anything else.

At the class, I was thrilled when Billy jumped right in, raising his hands to answer questions about the baby-care video
and volunteering for all the activities. During one event, all the
children gathered in a group to learn how to change a baby's
diaper. The instructor gave everyone a doll and a tiny dispos-
able diaper for them to practice with. Billy got into it, trying to
do his best, flipping the diaper around this way and that to find
the easiest fit.

David, however, came running up to me and sat beside
me, arms folded and scowling. "What's the matter, Dave?" I
asked.

Looking straight ahead, he replied, "I *don't* play with dolls."
I couldn't help grinning at his resolve. I explained to him that
it would help him take care of the baby, and it could be fun.
The instructor even came over to persuade David to give it a
try. David's stare stayed fixed on the same spot ahead of him
as he repeated, "I *don't* play with dolls." I apologized to the
instructor and let David sit there and sulk. I knew it wasn't
very politically correct for my son to be so appalled at the idea
of guys playing with dolls, but, hey, what could I do about it?
His father, after all, wasn't the most socially and domestically
enlightened man himself.

I turned my attention to Billy, who had suddenly trans-
formed into "Mr. Mom." He sprinkled baby powder into the
loose diaper on the doll and then picked up the baby, careful to
cradle its head just as the instructor had demonstrated earlier.

I shook my head in amusement, remembering how adamant he had once been about not wanting another sibling. I absolutely could not wait until the boys came to see their new brother at the hospital. They would both fall in love with him.

I remember the first time I had held Billy, our first child, how instantaneously Kevin and I bonded with him and how our connection had grown with each passing day. When I fed Billy during those first days, his eyes would look into mine and move from side to side, as if searching to find out who this stranger was. I could see his little soul beginning. Then, as he came to know me, he would still look into my eyes, but they weren't searching anymore. His eyes gazed into mine without darting from side to side. It was a look of trust, contentment, love, and the knowledge that I was there to take care of him. I wouldn't have traded that look for anything on this earth.

There is nothing like a newborn to refresh one's outlook on the world. Just before Jason was born, I visited my mother's cousin in a retirement home, where elderly people sat in wheel-chairs, a few moaning and others staring ahead, oblivious to everything. I was very self-conscious of my swollen, pregnant belly, a symbol of life beginning, while around me so many lives were approaching their terminus. I felt almost guilty to be in such a place, having something so new and wonderful to look forward to.

Then I noticed a number of the elderly people smiling at me, nodding as they looked at my stomach, reassuring me in their own way that life is meant to go on in its mysterious cycle of beginnings and endings. And at that moment, I felt my baby move inside me, also reminding me how very precious life is.

I promised myself, as I stood there in the retirement home

lounge, that the third time around I'd take time to appreciate those early years of motherhood. I knew the three a.m. feedings and the diaper changing wouldn't last forever, and that pretty soon he'd be out the door playing basketball in the cul-de-sac, not giving Mom a second thought. I promised myself I'd savor those moments with my baby and those moments with Billy and David, so I could remember them years in the future when the house would be empty and quiet; and then after this time of reminiscing, I could bask in the solitude, order in Chinese food, and read books all afternoon without a single Power Ranger toy in sight.

♦ He's Here!

If there were a fire at my house during the night and I could only save one family photo, which one would it be? (Moms, don't pretend you don't think about this hypothetical question because I know you do.) After the birth of our third son, I had the answer: it would be the photo of Billy, nine years old at the time, clearly in awe as he holds our newborn, Jason, while six-year-old David leans over Billy's shoulder, peering curiously down at the baby. The picture is remarkable in that it captures the older boys' feelings in that moment, and no matter how hard I may try, I know that no words I could ever string together would create the same effect.

Saying, "Here's your little brother!" to Billy and David as they entered my hospital room will go down as one of the most spectacular moments of my life. My husband's, too. The three of them belong together, and that third child, about whom my husband and I had debated for so long, the third child that I'd dreamed of, was a blessing to us all.

I went into labor about a week early while we were staying at my parents' house. The construction crew was still finishing up the family room addition at our home, so it became a crazy, stress-filled time as the construction took much longer than we'd planned (we had a porty-potty in our yard for over six months). On this particular day, Kevin was out of town for some meetings about two hours away. It was not the perfect time to have a baby, but I don't think the little guy was too concerned about that.

Around 6 p.m. my water broke, meaning I needed to get to the hospital quickly. Once those membranes break, the chance for infection to the baby increases. (Thank God this didn't happen two days earlier when I was sitting cautiously on the expensive silk sofa at an elderly relative's house; the thing was worth thousands of dollars, so I was relieved to get out of there before my amniotic sac ruined her antique furniture.)

I called Kevin, who was stuck in traffic on the interstate returning from his meeting. "I'll be there as soon as I can," he said when I told him I was on my way to the hospital. Since my mother wasn't sure about how to get to the birth center and I knew I wouldn't feel like yelling out directions during contractions, my father drove me in his station wagon.

On the way to the hospital, Daddy turned on the emergency flashers à la Barney Fife and wove us through the streets of Raleigh, all serious business, one mission on his mind. Once at the hospital, he went into the room with me, and a nurse hooked me up to monitors to read my blood pressure and check my baby's heart rate. As the familiar sound of the baby's heart began to fill the room, I turned to my father, who, despite having four children and soon, eight grandchildren, had never heard an unborn baby's heartbeat.

"Listen, Daddy," I whispered. I watched as my father smiled, surely struck by the same wonder I had felt nine years earlier when I heard Billy's heartbeat.

"Isn't that something?" he said. He was amazed. I could see it in his eyes, in the way he cocked his head, straining to listen to the delicate pulse. I was glad to share that miraculous sound with my father.

Then the nurse said she wanted to see how many centimeters I was. I turned to my father, who was seated in a chair at the end of my bed. "Uh, Daddy, you might want to move," I hinted.

"Huh?"

Obviously, he was a veteran of the waiting room when his own children were born, in the days when new dads were banished there while the delivery took place.

"I have to check her," the nurse said as she went to the bottom of the bed and started working under the sheets.

My father suddenly caught on and hopped up as if somebody had shouted, "Free cornbread and black-eyed peas in the lobby!"

"Whoa here!" he said and made a beeline for the door. I hadn't seen him move that fast in years.

As labor progressed, and Kevin finally arrived, the pain intensified, and I remembered from my first two deliveries that it only got worse. So I opted for an epidural, which is what I had done with my other boys. I seriously believe that the epidural inventor should be honored on a postage stamp, or, heck, maybe we should rename a state after him. Think about it.

Some mom is buying stamps, and the postman says, "Okay, we got the Muppets, a pink flower, some kind of bird, and the person who invented the epidural." Who's she going to choose? Talk about bringing in the bucks for the postal service.

It's a shame that the epidural inventor is not well-known. All of us women who have benefited from his contribution to medicine should be shouting his praises from the rooftops. Most Internet sites credit Dr. John J. Bonica as the person who invented the epidural block. Before it was widely used in childbirth, he gave it to his own wife when she was in labor with their second child (do I hear any nominations for Husband of the Millennium?). February 16th is his birthday, and I propose that we declare this a national holiday complete with fireworks and pain-numbing medications for all women in celebration of Bonica's accomplishment. I envision a grassroots movement, here, ladies.

It took a while for my contractions to become regular and then grow stronger. By this time, Kevin had finally made it to the hospital, and he stood by the bed, gripping my hand when the pain and the pushing got to be too much. One shift ended and another one began as two doctors traded places in our room. Ironically, the new doc happened to be the young man who had assumed my childbearing years were over several years ago. "It figures," Kevin mumbled when he saw the doctor walk in the door.

After midnight, Jason was born, crying that precious newborn shriek that sounds like part lion cub and part bleating goat. I held him and comforted him, and his crying tapered off. He was sleeping in my arms as Kevin and I took in every detail about him.

Our third son. There was no disappointment at all, just overwhelming joy in welcoming this beautiful baby boy into the world, complete thankfulness that we were blessed to be his parents. I'd gladly buy Power Rangers again instead of Barbies. I admit the thought shot through my mind that he was born three days after the age cut-off date in Little League baseball. Oh well, I'd worry about that when he was five.

My parents brought Billy and David to the hospital a little while later, the boys each wearing big, round "I'm a Big Brother" buttons on their chests. A few moments later that picture of our three boys was taken, a picture I will keep somewhere on my bookshelf, as well as imbedded in my heart, for the rest of my life.

Later, when the boys kissed the baby's forehead and began arguing over whose turn it was to hold him, I knew Jason would fit into our family just fine.

◆ "Are You Going to Try for a Girl?"

"Are y'all going to try for a girl?" a well-meaning friend asked only a few weeks after our third son was born. I cringed. I'd just gotten through labor and delivery less than a month earlier. Back off, woman. Yet, this is the inevitable question that parents of only boys come to expect. We take it good-naturedly, but after a while, I gotta tell you—I feel like wrapping my fingers around the neck of the next person who asks it and squeezing like a boa constrictor on steroids.

We've all seen those families that obviously tried for a girl. They are the families we see rambling through the mall or occupying both sides of the Golden Corral buffet line at once; they're comprised of the parents, three or four sons, and the prized daughter wearing patent leather shoes and a frilly dress—the youngest of the children. You can bet your 401K that they tried for a girl, and at last, they got her. God bless that mom for not giving up and going back to the well time after time, boy after boy. Admittedly, that mother is more of a woman than I. But she's a lunatic, too. Even with her daughter providing a little extra estrogen, their house is still going to be drenched in testosterone, what with all the sons it took to get one daughter.

Of course, let's remember that each of those boys she had was a welcome and joyous addition to the family, regardless of their gender; I'd hate for little boys to ever get the idea that they are second best. No way. Sometimes moms would just like a bit of balance in the household levels of testosterone and estrogen, and so some choose to take a deep breath and forge ahead in trying for a daughter.

To be honest, Kevin and I *did* try for a girl the second time around but were given David instead. (Perhaps I shouldn't mention this to him or he might get some kind of complex... It's okay, honey, we still love you.) I'd heard about those methods of timing sex to increase your chances of having a boy or a girl, and we decided to try it. We already had one boy, so we thought it would be neat to have one of each, to even things up in the house—okay, maybe it was just me who thought this. It wasn't that we didn't want a boy, but we decided if there was a way to increase the probability of a sperm with an X chromosome meeting up with the egg instead of one with a Y, we'd give it a shot.

Those methods of sex determination of the baby depend on the frequency and time of the month a couple has sex. The gender selection manual said if you want a girl, try to conceive a day or so after ovulation instead of immediately after (as if I know the exact moment—I can't even keep track of what year to write on my checks) because the X sperm live longer than the Y's, thereby increasing the chance of having a girl. For a boy, the rule was to have sex as soon as you know you're ovulating because male Y sperm travel faster than X ones, and there will be more of them reaching the egg first.

The frequency thing was something about having sex less often if you want a girl or, wait a minute…maybe it was more. Hell, I don't remember, although I do recall some guy in our prenatal class when I was pregnant with Billy who said trying to conceive a particular gender was like "feast or famine" when it came to sex. It's funny how a bunch of strangers come together in these classes and are soon talking about their personal sex lives as though they're on *The Jerry Springer Show*. Pregnancy has a certain kind of liberating power.

There was something about the optimal position to do it in, but, thank God, that information seems to have been erased from my brain. All of this exact method stuff became laughable for us; we rarely had time to ourselves as it was, much less time to schedule our sex life around sporadic ovulation cycles. Basically, a realistic goal for me was simply to find two hours to catch a movie before it hit the video stores. But we attempted to have a girl anyway because some of my friends had followed these gender selection rules, and their babies all turned out to be the desired sex.

Not so with us. Of course, I never was really good at following directions, especially when this stuff was kind of like advanced math, probability and all, and by far my weakest subject.

So with Jason we didn't worry about "the method." It seemed no matter when or how our babies were conceived, it was a sure bet, they were going to be boys. I don't think Kevin is capable of producing anything except Y chromosome sperm. A couple of times while I was pregnant with Jason, I had this strange dream where the inside of Kevin's body was actually a stage for one of those weird MTV videos. There were thousands of actors dressed as the letter Y running everywhere, dancing to "Macho Man" by the Village People. Y's everywhere. Y's disco dancing on stage, their pointer fingers jutting toward the sky in rhythm to the beat, each step choreographed to perfection. And not a single blankety-blank letter X to be found. I didn't need a psychologist to interpret that dream for me. If we had ten babies, there would still be no girls. That's just the way it is with some couples.

Before we knew whether Jason would be a boy or a girl, I imagined our third child as a quiet, well-behaved little girl who would sit silently and play with dolls or color between the lines in a Little Pony activity book. Her daddy would adore her and cater to her every whim, at last gaining a true appreciation of the female sex and, thereby, making my own life a bit easier. That is indeed one reason I wanted to have a girl: I thought it would "soften" Kevin a bit and help put him in touch with his sensitive side and see life through the eyes of a—dare I say it?—female. I was kind of tired of sitting down at the breakfast table where the guys would promptly raise their orange juice glasses in the air and toast aloud: "To men!" Sad to say, folks, but I'm not joking here. They also used to call me "Shemale," a mispronunciation of *female*, which my husband used in conversation with the boys, like, "Go tell the Shemale it's time to leave."

As Jason grew into toddlerhood, there was no doubt he was another rough-and-tumble boy, the same as my other two. I was hoping he would be my calm, thoughtful child, allowing me to write at the computer or read without watching him every second to keep him from killing himself. But he turned out to be more active than Billy and David were at that age, climbing all over furniture, wrestling on the floor with his brothers as if he were just as big as them. He had to learn to take up for himself, and he eventually developed a better left hook than anybody in the family.

Since I had wanted a third child desperately, while Kevin had to be coaxed into it, it was me who had to pay the proverbial price. I was the one who stayed at home with hyper Jason all day, as Kevin escaped to the office. Sometimes I suspected God was up there smiling, maybe winking at my husband, slapping him a holy high-five. "I don't think she'll want a fourth," the Big Guy would say to Kevin, both of them chuckling.

There's no chance of us having a fourth child, though. When Jason wasn't even a month old, Kevin decided to get the "V-word," as men call it. They can't bring themselves to say it, don't have the strength to muster the word. It's VASECTOMY, guys. V-A-S-E-C-T-O-M-Y. If women can handle labor and episiotomies, you guys can handle *vasectomy*, okay?

Prior to the procedure, Kevin's doctor gave him valium for the "pain" and even said it was okay to have a drink or two before coming to the office. "No way," I said to Kevin, after he told me those were the doctor's instructions. He showed them to me scribbled in the doctor's handwriting. I did a double take, not believing my eyes, and looked again. Yep, he was telling the truth—valium and alcohol. I never got valium after any of my three deliveries. Hell, I thought, *I* want a vasectomy! Men act as though undergoing a vasectomy is the most terrible thing imaginable and visibly flinch when the word is mentioned, yet they get to take valium and alcohol to ease them through it. Meanwhile, the wife has to wait on him and take care of the kids while he lies in bed or on the couch, watching ESPN and CNN, icing his manhood. Hmmm, the only V-word that comes to my mind is *vacation.*

Kevin was so relaxed when he went in for his "procedure" that the loose-fitting sweat pants he was advised to wear kept sliding down his butt, and he didn't even care. I, on the other hand, was totally embarrassed as I trailed along behind him trying to provide some cover. I was half hoping we wouldn't run into any of his clients and half hoping we would, just to see Kevin's reaction. Of course, he was so out of it that he probably wouldn't have cared who he happened to encounter. He wouldn't remember a thing the next day anyway. Then again, he never remembered a damn thing even when he was coherent.

While checking in at the front desk, he started singing a song he made up about all the little spermies going swimming away. And folks, Kevin does *not* normally express himself in song. But on this day he could have starred in a Broadway musical.

So we sat there with the other couples as all the men in the room held their little brown bags filled with their samples. I hoped I wouldn't see anybody I knew, like the middle school principal or somebody from church. It might be sort of hard to make small talk in such a situation. "Hey there, Bob, whatcha got in the bag?"

Then I started thinking about the way Kevin and I must look in the waiting room with three-week-old Jason sleeping in his carrier, the two of us there with a newborn baby. Strangers probably thought we were a couple hitting forty who just had their first child, and after a drastic lifestyle change with three weeks of no sleep, constant crying, and dirty diapers, we decided to make sure this wouldn't ever happen again and rushed to the nearest V-doctor for the Big Snip. Or maybe a small snip depending on one's perspective. In any case, a few parents in the office kept offering me baby-care advice as if they thought we must be really struggling. I guess we appeared rather desperate. My stress was simply over Kevin's sliding pants and worrying about whether he'd strike up another verse of the spermie song.

So from that day on, this is my true, heartfelt, unequivocal answer to everyone's question: No, we're not going to try for a girl. Really. We're not. Really.

◆ Nature, Not Nurture

Guys are guys pretty much from the start. There might be a little bit of learned behavior, but for the most part, they're slobs and hooter-lovers right out of the womb. More nature than nurture, though believe me, I'm doing my best to inject a little culture and sensitivity into my sons' masculinity syndromes.

I can't tell you the number of times I've embarked on a cleaning adventure behind my couch and found so much junk back there that our family room could've been rezoned as a city dump; sticky lollipops, moldy milk cups, toy wrappers, wadded-up paper towels, and crunchy bits of bagel are just a few of the treasures I've discovered.

To be fair, I have to say that Billy is quite neat, but he "straightens up" more than he actually cleans. Who can blame the kid for not wanting to live in a pigpen like his brothers? However, one problem is he sometimes straightens up piles of my important papers, which I have laid out in an accessible place because of that very importance, and I end up losing half of them.

David is the messy one. Several years ago there was a night when I went to lie beside him on his bed because he couldn't fall asleep, and I woke up with my legs and back covered in chewed bubble gum. David had a habit of leaving wads of gum in unlikely places if a trash can wasn't convenient. Because of this difference in their approach to cleanliness, Billy and David are at each other's throats relentlessly, with Billy barking out orders to David, who ignores them.

Kevin picks up like Billy does. He considers cleaning up as throwing stuff in cabinets, not scrubbing or dusting. Real cleaning has to be repeated so frequently in our house that I've become a bit slack about doing it myself. It's frustrating to spend all day cleaning up only to have the house become filthy forty-eight hours later. I read one time that harried housewives shouldn't worry if there are toys strewn about on the floor of their home or papers stacked on the kitchen table because there's a difference between simply having a messy house and having a dirty one. I often wonder, though, if our house has crossed that line.

Another thing that boys do right out of the starting gate at an early age is pay unwarranted attention to the male sex organ. When my boys were toddlers, they constantly put their hands down there and felt around, prompting me to panic and drag them into the bathroom, thinking they had to pee when they didn't. (And what is it with guys and peeing? They pass the age of ten, and suddenly their stream hitting the toilet sounds like Niagara Falls cascading over the rocks).

When Billy was two, he became alarmed when he happened to see me step out of the shower and noticed that I was missing a penis. Accustomed to going to Toys "Я" Us or Wal-Mart for his heart's every desire, he went to his dad and said, "I want to go to the store to buy Mommy a penis." At first Kevin just about choked from laughing so hard, but afterward he explained to Billy that Mommy was not as "lucky" as they were. To guys, the male organ is essentially the key to all the power in the world, and anybody lacking one is from a strange, deprived species indeed. It never crossed Billy's mind (or Kevin's) that Mommy might like to have something else from the store instead, such as jewelry or a new frying pan or anything else in the whole damn place.

I also remember Jason's surprise when I explained to him that boys stand up to pee, but girls sit down. He looked at me as if I'd just said they wouldn't be making any more Oreos. Disbelief. Total shock. He must have asked me twenty times that day when I would "grow" one. These kind of questions come up regularly in a household that has boys and only one woman who must go about her normal life while her sons constantly observe her. Early explanations of tampons involve gentle tact and changing the subject. (Though I do make an effort with our oldest guys to make sure they will someday appreciate that women have to suffer through "the curse.")

Then there's that question moms of boys everywhere dread—the one boys ask as perplexed preschoolers just waking and getting out of bed in the morning: "Mom, why won't my penis go down?" I wish these kinds of sensitive biological processes wouldn't happen until later in life when boys have an understanding of what's going on—or that they would at least ask their fathers first. That way, poor moms wouldn't have to stutter and stammer their way through any sort of fanciful explanation.

Our best "male organ" story was when David was five and had to have a dark freckle removed from his bottom. For the outpatient surgery, they prescribed David codeine to take beforehand (a precursor, I guess, to taking valium before vasectomies), which they said was very strong and would make him go to sleep. Well, it didn't. So they gave him some more, unaware it was having the exact opposite effect on David, as it does on most kids. He was totally wired, running from one side of the waiting room to the other and slamming into the wall, which gave literal meaning to the cliché "bouncing off the walls." Finally, he relaxed a little but still wasn't sleepy. The doctors decided to go for it anyway.

During the procedure, David was awake but looked woozy. As he was lying there, he put his hand under the sheet, and then turned his head to us and grinned. "I feel my weinke," he said gleefully. I made a belated attempt to drown out his words by coughing. But the nurses had heard and were stifling smiles.

Now I ask you: would a little girl do something like that? Absolutely not. I could hear David sometime in the distant future singing the spermie song as he held that precious little brown bag at the doctor's office. I made a mental note to warn his wife.

And then, of course, there is the natural breast fixation that most guys seem to have. It comes straight from the womb, folks. I can attest to that. I breastfed all of my boys—Billy and David for just a little over a year and Jason for more than two. I was beginning to think I'd have to pry Jason off with a crowbar in order to wean him. He was like a bulldog with a bone. I hope he doesn't grow up to be one of those guys who ogle girls' boobs all the time, nudging his friends and saying, "Hey, man, check out that pair." During my years of breastfeeding, Kevin said many times about each of the boys: "He's definitely a breast man."

When Billy was about one year old, the three of us were in York, Maine, visiting Kevin's great aunt Kay, who was in her late eighties. We took Aunt Kay to eat one night at a seafood restaurant high up on the cliffs near a famous lighthouse. As the waitress was going through her rundown of the daily specials, Billy was evidently becoming intrigued by the lighthouse embroidered on the left pocket of her shirt. Just as she was telling us about the lobster casserole, Billy reached out and squeezed the lighthouse on her shirt, pinching it between his fingers. Unfortunately, he grabbed a handful of breast, too. The girl's face immediately turned red as did ours as we admonished Billy for being so rude. Yet, he was a baby. I mean, what are you going to do? The boy liked lighthouses. But looking back and knowing what I do now about males, I believe he had an ulterior motive in mind.

The waitress, poor thing, was a good sport about it all.

(I should have told her to get used to having her boobs squished because this was nothing compared to a mammogram.) When Kevin mentioned that he couldn't wait to tell his cousin what happened, Aunt Kay, without missing a beat or cracking a grin, replied, "Yes, dear, you'll have to keep him *abreast* of the situation."

Breastfeeding was an incredible bonding experience for my sons and me. I honestly enjoyed it, except for the time I got stuck in a breast pump just after I'd bought it. I'd forgotten to put in some kind of little suction release valve in the nipple plates. Let me tell you—that little valve is a very essential part of a properly functioning breast pump. I turned the machine on, and there was this loud sucking noise like Moses was using a huge Hoover vacuum cleaner to drain the Red Sea, but some fleshy sea creature had gotten stuck in it instead. The sound droned on while I frantically tried to free myself from the pump's airtight seal. I searched for the on/off switch but couldn't locate it, so I yanked the plastic tubing out of the unit, sending milk droplets squirting everywhere. Luckily, there wasn't any harm done. Physically, anyway, but emotionally...well, let's just say if I'm ever arrested for doing anything violent, I think I could use this incident in my defense.

Yet what I recall most vividly about the breastfeeding years of my life was the weekend I went away. It was the first time I'd left Billy, who was three months old, overnight with Kevin, and I had mixed feelings about it. I was excited to be going with a college buddy to a good friend's wedding four hours away, but I worried about leaving my son. Plus, pumping enough milk to leave behind for him and being hooked up to the tubes and bottles made me feel like Ol' Bessie at milking time.

After filling a notebook of precise baby instructions for Kevin; arranging baby clothes, medicine, and food in the proper places; writing down doctors' numbers by the phone; and packing for myself, I was finally ready to leave.

As we drove across North Carolina to the seaside town where the wedding would take place, my friend Amy shouted over the radio, "I can't wait to hit the beach!" She glanced at me. "How about you?"

"I'm just looking forward to sleeping through the night," I told her. She giggled the carefree laugh of a single woman who hadn't yet experienced getting up with a baby at three o'clock in the morning.

I was the matron of honor and had to be there on time, but we encountered some traffic delays and began to get nervous about possibly being late. I still had to change from my jeans and T-shirt into the dress I'd bought for the rehearsal. When we finally exited off the highway and out of the traffic, I punched the gas, zooming down the two-lane road toward the coast. The old highway seemed endless, its flat stretches running on forever into the haze. I knew we weren't going to make it in time.

At last we reached the small, rustic church, arriving twenty minutes late. It had been hours since I'd last breastfed Billy, and I was—how should I put it—about to pop. Unfortunately, there was no time to pull out the breast pump. We rushed into the church and searched for a restroom to change in but couldn't find one. A side door to the sanctuary was ajar, and we peeked in to see a very reserved, well-dressed wedding party already taking instructions from the minister. I was now desperate to find a place to change.

I ducked into the dimly lit janitor's closet, feeling like Clark Kent in a phone booth trying to put on his cape. I pulled off my jeans and put on my blue floral sundress. No mirror for a final check; the outfit would just have to do. However, when I had picked out the moderately revealing dress at the store, I hadn't just gone seven hours without breastfeeding. This didn't cross my mind, though, until I stepped out of the janitor's closet into the hallway where Amy was waiting. She turned and stared at me.

"Where did you get *those?*" Amy asked, her eyes wider than I'd ever seen them. I caught a glimpse of myself in a hallway mirror, cleavage bulging out of my suddenly tight-fitting dress. We doubled over in laughter, bringing our friend, Michelle, the bride, out to see what was going on.

"Whoa!" she shouted, upon seeing the newly enhanced me. When I entered the sanctuary, members of the wedding party did double-takes as I walked toward the group. Then the elbow nudges and whispering started. In less than a minute, rumors were going around that I'd had a boob job. "Hey," I wanted to tell them, "they may be temporary, but they're 100 percent *real.*" I contemplated for a moment whether to keep a breast pump in the closet for the rest of my life; voila! Boobs-on-demand.

As I practiced my exit down the aisle, the groom's brother started singing, "Double Shot of My Baby's Love," prompting snickers from the wedding party. The situation was a bit embarrassing, but having never been the center of attention for this particular reason before, I decided to enjoy it. I did notice, however, that when the solemn minister caught his first glimpse of me in my lower-cut-than-was-appropriate-for-a-wedding dress, he furrowed his eyebrows in what I deemed to be a disapproving look. I made a point of mentioning to him later—nonchalantly, of course—that I taught Sunday school and was on a committee at my church. But I think my attempt to salvage his impression of me was a lost cause.

I felt like a cross between Dolly Parton, Jezebel, and Cinderella at the ball, waiting for the clock to strike midnight. I knew this wasn't going to last long, and it might be wise to leave the church a little early, which I did. Didn't want to spring a leak.

Later, when Michelle told me the rehearsal photos didn't turn out, I was disappointed my "big" moment hadn't been captured on film. What a waste of pregnancy's fringe benefits. I promised myself the next time I went this long without breastfeeding that I'd take advantage of the situation and "accidentally" run into an old boyfriend. And I would know, as he stared at my breasts, that he couldn't help himself. He was a guy. It was a God-given trait of males, straight from the womb.

2

The Guy Zone: Those Who Goeth Never Returneth

— Sure Signs You're the Mother of Boys —

+ You have to chase down the family dog to retrieve your son's jock strap.

+ If you lined up all the ball caps scattered across your house, they would stretch longer than the line for the women's restroom at a Michael Bolton concert.

+ They think PMS is the new Play Station video game system.

+ There's an air hockey table where your dining room table should be.

+ You can't get your car in the garage because of all the sports equipment.

+ You realize you are the only one in the house who can remember a damn thing.

+ You realize you are the only one in the house who can find a damn thing.

+ You sneak out of the house just to have meaningful conversations with other women.

✦ The Guy Zone

There's a place in our solar system that defies all logic, a place where all common sense and the ability to pay attention dissolve into the atmosphere. It's a place I like to call "The Guy Zone." This is the realm in which guys fall inexplicably into a deep, dark chasm and cannot be reached by reasonable human beings, also known as women.

One of the first times in my life I became aware of this phenomenon was a few months after Kevin and I were married, and we attended the wedding of one of his college buddies. On the way to the wedding, Kevin told me about the reception plans and then mentioned the couple was going to Cancun, Mexico, for their honeymoon, where they would stay in a very posh resort.

Later, when I was standing in the receiving line after the ceremony, I was trying to think of something to say to the bride other than the trite "best wishes." When our turn came, Kevin shook his friend's hand and gave the bride a peck on the cheek. Then I gave her a quick hug, told her the wedding was beautiful and added, "I know you can't wait to get to Cancun!" Her smile froze, and her eyes glazed over. The groom looked mortified. But the people behind us in line leaned in to offer their congratulations, which switched the couple's focus to them. Kevin put his hand on my back and guided me ahead.

"What was the matter with them?" I asked, perplexed.

Kevin winced. "Well, he was kind of keeping the location of the honeymoon a secret from her. It was kind of a surprise."

"*What?*" I screamed. I felt sick.

"Calm down. It's over with now. Nothing you can do about it."

I pushed Kevin's hands off my shoulder. "You knew Cancun

was a secret, and you left out that one tiny little detail when you told me about it?"

"Who knew you'd bring it up?"

"Who knew I wouldn't? It's a very strange thing to leave out something so important."

He shrugged. "I didn't think about it."

Ah-ha. There are the five little words with which I've become so familiar throughout our many years of marriage—"I didn't think about it."

The other phrase I hear all too often is, "Oh, yeah." As in, "Kevin, why did you plan the big Scout camping trip for that weekend? That's the weekend you're supposed to be in your cousin's wedding party."

Kevin pauses, stares into space, looking like the English language is making sense to him for the first time in his life and says with wonder in his voice, "Oh yeah." It's as if an invisible barrier that had surrounded him his entire life suddenly crumbles to the ground, allowing a brief moment of enlightenment, before being built up again.

It's the guy zone, ladies—a scientific theory that will be proven in this century.

Billy, our eldest, used to be my companion in laughing or complaining about all the silly things my husband does—such as not remembering a conversation about something that everyone else seems to recall. There were times Kevin would say to me, "You didn't tell me about that."

"Yes, I did," I would reply.

"No, you didn't."

I'd pause for a moment to replay the conversation in question in my mind. Yes, it had happened. "Don't you remember?"

I would ask. "It was Thursday night after David's baseball game, and we were driving home." He'd stare at me blankly, while I began to question my own sanity.

And then Billy, God bless him, would come to my rescue. "Yeah, Dad, she told you that. I heard her. It was in the car." Having a witness is always a good thing. A requirement if you're married to a man who has testosterone-induced Alzheimer's.

Billy and I were also observers of my husband's inability to locate a single, ordinary object that I asked him to find, whether it was in the kitchen, garage, closet, or grocery store. The guy zone is as amazing as it is frustrating. I can't count the number of times Kevin would swear up and down that an item wasn't in the pantry where I had told him to look. Take, for instance, a can of vegetable soup. "It's not here," Kevin would insist, as he stood like a statue in front of the kitchen pantry, never bothering to lean over and take a closer look or move cans around in his search. He'd peer into the rows of cans and bags of snacks as if he thought the soup can would raise up arms and wave at him. "Yoo-hoo, over here by the green beans!"

Then Billy or I would stand beside him, glance into the pantry, and pluck the "missing" item right in front of him. "Oh," he'd mumble. "I didn't see it." Billy and I would exchange knowing glances and shake our heads in exasperation as Kevin walked to get the can opener, unaware of our obvious irritation.

I was always so glad to have Billy's sympathetic support and testimony during these times when my husband descended into the guy zone.

But I fear those days have come to an end. During Billy's early teen years, he began to display some of his father's "you didn't tell me that" and "I don't see it" traits. I tried not to believe it at first, but there was no denying it. Billy wasn't my little boy any longer. He was becoming a "guy." Like it or not, boys start doing more guy things as they get older.

Billy still tells me play-by-play of moments in Red Sox games and verbatim dialogue from every episode of *The Simpsons* or any James Bond movie. Yet, if I'm yearning for meaningful conversation or details of real events in his life, I'm left to scrounge for crumbs.

Several years ago after a seventh-grade dance, this exercise in futility became obvious. I picked Billy up in the carpool line, and he hopped in the back seat. We exchanged hellos and then sat in the traffic without talking. I knew he had information that I wanted about the dance, but I also knew he'd get perturbed, as most males do, about my asking questions. But I decided to risk it anyway.

"So did ya dance?" I asked.

He mumbled something that sounded like "yeah." My heart soared.

"So you just walked up and asked her?"

"No."

As someone who lives with four males, I knew this meant I had to interpret his answer, to connect the dots. "You mean *she* asked you?"

I glanced in the rearview mirror and noticed a slight smile tug at the corners of his lips. "Yeah."

I was eager to garner every possible scrap of information, but I had to play it cool. "That's nice," I said, as I watched a group of giggling girls get in the car ahead of us. I could see them through the window, chattering away with the mom as soon as they climbed inside. I felt a stab of pain. The carpool line started crawling forward. "Who was she?" This time I tried to sound casual.

"I'd never seen her before."

I paused, giving him time between questions. "So what'd she look like?"

"I dunno," Billy muttered.

I sensed my window of opportunity closing. "You don't know what she looked like?" I repeated.

He scoffed. "It was dark, Mom."

"How do you know you didn't recognize her if it was that dark?" No answer. Sighing, I decided to try again. "What was her name?" I asked, as I watched all the females in the other car laughing and having a grand time gossiping and exchanging details.

He shrugged. "I dunno."

"She didn't tell you her name?"

"Yeah, she did but—" he paused. Then I realized it was not a pause at all; he'd simply stopped talking and let his sentence dangle there in mid-air. My curiosity was piqued, to say the least.

"But what?"

"I didn't hear her." I glanced at him in the mirror, then looked away, shaking my head in frustration.

"It was loud," he said.

Right. As if that was an adequate explanation, and as if I was going to buy it.

So far I knew it was dark and it was loud, supposedly. I felt like an FBI interrogator trying to get a confession out of somebody. That's when I realized this conversation seemed all too familiar. It was the kind of "pulling teeth" talk I'd often had with—a chill ran down my spine at this point—my husband.

Suddenly, I wanted to reach over the back seat, grab my son, and yank him back from the abyss. I almost screamed, "Billy, Billy, come back to me!" Yet I knew it was too late. He was already slipping over the edge, into the vast wasteland known as the guy zone.

✦ "I Can Fix It Myself"

For a lot of men, calling upon an expert to solve a problem is a way of admitting failure or defeat, so they frequently try to defend themselves and their manhood by uttering a second set of five familiar words: "I can fix it myself." (Remember, all you single ladies and newlyweds: Men live by simple creeds and mottos. By realizing this early on, perhaps you can sneak something like, "Let the experts handle it," into their repertoire of manly phrases.)

I grew up hearing, "I can fix it myself," from my fabulous father, a mechanical engineering grad, who, like McGyver, can repair anything, even if he has nothing but duct tape and paper clips. He's always had a lot of ingenuity and has even invented and patented a successful ruffling machine for the sewing industry.

I don't doubt the man's brilliance, but I've also seen how frustrating his go-it-alone exploits have sometimes been to my mother when he'd rig up an unsightly contraption attached to the toilet, so it could flush without overflowing. He'd spend hours "perfecting" such an innovation.

Despite being impressed with my father's knowledge, I secretly vowed to marry a man who would simply pick up a phone and call the professionals—the plumbers, carpenters, landscapers, and electricians of the world, God love 'em.

Instead, I have Kevin. He, like my father, insists on doing the fix-it projects around our house on his own. When I first told my mother this soon after I got married, she sighed, shook her head, and looked forlorn. She knew what I was in for.

One of the problems with a do-it-yourselfer is that it takes a while for him to actually get around to doing it. Sure, I know they're busy, but that's the whole point of *calling somebody else!!!*

Awhile back, I was downstairs in the kitchen and happened to notice there was a rust-colored stain on our stucco ceiling—right below the toilet in our sons' bathroom upstairs. I'd actually suspected the leak a few days earlier when I saw some water around the toilet base. I told Kevin my suspicions, but he downplayed them. Now, here was my proof—a big, ugly stain.

Kevin went upstairs to take care of the problem. When he was all done, I went up to take a look. There was a blue towel wrapped around the toilet base. "Can I pick that up now?" I asked.

Kevin shook his head. "I think I fixed the problem, but the towel will still have to stay there just in case."

Thoughts of my father came zooming into my mind. "For how long?"

"Probably forever," he replied.

I dropped my head, then peered at him to make sure he wasn't teasing. He wasn't. I was incredulous. "Or..." I paused, trying to select my wording carefully because I knew this was delicate territory for some men. "Or you could just call a plumber."

And there it was on his face. The "you just offended my manhood" look.

"I can do it myself just fine," Kevin protested.

"Yep," I said and glanced at the towel on the floor. "You did it yourself all right."

"What's that supposed to mean?" Kevin asked.

"I just wish that once in a while we could go through the *Yellow Pages* like most people and call somebody who knows what they're doing." Oops. The words spewed out of my mouth before I could stop them.

He looked hurt, like one of our sons after striking out in Little League. "You don't think I know what I'm doing?"

I shrugged my shoulders, then gestured toward the towel. I thought the evidence spoke pretty well for itself.

Undeterred, Kevin said, "Is there water on the floor?"

I surveyed the area. "Well, no."

"Then the problem is fixed." He strode out of the bathroom, leaving me open-mouthed and staring at the towel.

There was another time when the dryer stopped working because the door wouldn't close. Until Kevin had time to look at the problem, we had to use the old standby, duct tape, which didn't work very well. Crunched for time, Kevin actually told me to look in the phone book and find a repairman. I was absolutely giddy as I flipped through the *Yellow Pages*. It's not normal to derive so much excitement from getting an appliance repaired.

Alas, it was too good to be true. Kevin had some sort of epiphany about how to fix the dryer. He had been upstairs studying the dryer and said confidently that he knew what to do. He was a man on a mission. The result was two trips to the store to buy a metal latch each time (the first one broke) and an exorbitant amount of time spent installing the first latch and then the second.

Then there was the time when Jason was four, and I took his Spiderman bike to the cycling shop to have new training wheels put on it. Kevin had been promising to fix the bike for months, telling us the wheels just needed to be "adjusted." But the training wheels were lopsided, and the metal bars connecting them to the main wheels were bent, making safety a definite issue. This wasn't a simple adjustment—tighten a few bolts and you're done. Jason was going to be too big to ride the damn thing pretty soon, and I knew we'd better get it repaired pronto or the wheels might just collapse.

Then Jason asked me, as he did occasionally, "Mommy, when can I ride my bike again?" The bike, which had been a Christmas gift, was all warped out of shape by the spring and remained in the garage in this derelict condition for six months. The poor kid would probably have hit puberty before his dad got around to fixing the training wheels.

I knew I couldn't wait on Kevin any longer; I had to take matters into my own hands. I decided to take the bike to the shop the next morning while Kevin was at work. Problem was, he's self-employed, so he can make his own schedule and come back home when he wants. The next morning, just as I was going out to the garage to put the bike in the back of the car, Kevin called me on his cell phone to tell me he was on his way home to get some papers he'd left behind.

Trying not to arouse suspicion, I told him I had some

errands to run and wouldn't be home. Then I raced out to the garage, popped open the back of our SUV, grabbed the bike, and jammed it in the rear compartment. A handlebar caught on the side, and I had to twist the bike to make it fit. I thought I heard Kevin's car coming down the street and turned to look, but it was just a neighbor. False alarm. I was nervous and moved quickly, feeling like a bike thief who might be pounced on by the law at any second. Ridiculous? Yes, I know, but I was directly violating the sacred "fix it" code, and if my husband discovered my plot, he might pull the bike out of the car, saying, "I'll get to it soon, honey." I broke out in a cold sweat and wrestled the damn bike into the car.

Luckily, I was already pulling out of the driveway when I saw Kevin driving up the street toward me. I waved to him, smiled, and never hit the brakes. A week later, Kevin seemed oblivious to the fact that Jason was suddenly riding his bike again.

Another thing that broke at our house was the wall-mounted telephone. I know most people have gone cordless and mobile and cellular and all that, but I am adamant about having at least one phone still attached to the wall. (At our house, that's the only way we can be sure we can even find a phone when it rings since the cordless ones are always lost, buried, or have dead batteries.) But the entire phone fell off the wall and crashed to the floor one day when Kevin passed by and hit it with his shoulder. At first there was no dial tone, but then Kevin fiddled with it for a few minutes with a screwdriver as though he were Alexander Graham Bell himself. He fixed it so we could dial out again, but we always had to hit the "tone" button first. To Kevin, because the phone was now usable, this meant it was fixed. Whenever I mentioned getting it properly repaired, he'd

reply, "Just hit tone." My point, however, was we weren't supposed to have to hit "tone." This was more than a nuisance to
me; I wondered what would happen if we had an emergency at
our house and a friend had to call 911 but couldn't get through
because they didn't hit "tone" first. Yeah, only a mother could
worry about a scenario like this, but it's possible.

I know not all men inherit this exasperating "I can fix it
myself" syndrome, but unfortunately for me, the ones in my
life did. So when Father's Day comes around again, I can tell
you what my husband and dad will *not* be receiving: not a tool-
box, not a power tool, and not a Home Depot gift certificate,
for these things would only encourage them.

And they wonder why they always get ties.

✦ Molding Men

THE PRESCHOOL TEACHER'S note came home in Jason's backpack one day. It read: "Please talk with Jason about name-
calling. It's becoming a distraction in class. Thanks!" I noticed
the word "please" was underlined. I was upset and disappointed with my youngest son and embarrassed for what I
deemed to be my failure as a parent. My husband and I had
heard "moron" and "idiot" become staples in Jason's growing
vocabulary (thanks to the teasing that always involved my two
oldest boys and husband), and I had taken disciplinary action,
but it obviously wasn't enough.

With my older two boys, I'd never received notes from a
teacher about their behavior; they had their ugly, reckless
moments at home, of course, but they also knew to behave at

school. For some reason, this bit of etiquette had eluded our youngest.

I looked at Jason as he sipped his apple juice and colored in his Scooby-Doo coloring book. He was a picture of total concentration, his blue eyes focused on his work, his bangs flipped up off his forehead. My heart sank as I put his backpack on the hanger and thought about the note. I went over and sat beside him.

"Jason, did you get in trouble at school today?" I asked. I tried to take it slow and use caution.

He kept coloring, not looking at me. "No."

"Are you sure?"

Still coloring. "Uh-huh."

"Well, your teacher sent a note saying you call people names. What did you call them?"

He sighed. "Okay, okay, I called this boy a toilet-head."

I hate to admit it, but my first reaction was relief. At least the name was more silly than mean, not his preferred "moron" or "idiot." I launched into a lecture about not saying bad words and respecting people's feelings. "I know you're a good boy, Jason, and I know you can act better than that." He agreed he would, and we hugged.

The second note came home a week later with the same plea, and the next day when I picked up Jason at school, I asked the teacher what Jason had said. This time it was "butthead." Uh-oh.

I was furious with Jason. I had never, ever come near washing any of my sons' mouths out with soap, but he was pushing me to reassess my limits. I dragged Jason, crying, into the bathroom and squirted a tiny bit of liquid soap onto his finger and then put his finger into his mouth—enough for him to get a taste but not feel sick. He screamed and cried and I finally let him take sips of water to rinse out his mouth. After that, I sent him to his room. He had gotten the message this time, surely.

For a week or two, things were fine. No more notes. Then, one day when I went to pick him up from school, the teacher took me aside and said it had happened again. This time the word was "big-mouth." I'd never heard him say that in my life. The teacher said she just wanted to make me aware of it, but that it wasn't anything to worry about; it was just part of Jason's learning process, his socialization.

I understood what she meant, but it was difficult not to be concerned about it. It got to the point that whenever I picked up Jason, I rushed to get him and get out of there before the teachers called me over to tell me about his latest outburst.

In previous preschool classes, Jason's teachers had not complained to me about his name-calling problem, but I was aware of a few other times when he would shout names at his brothers in public or call other kids "moron" when they would run into him on the soccer field or basketball court. There was even one time in the fall of 2004 when this happened while we were at the National D-Day Museum in Virginia, getting a tour from an elderly man who had actually served in World War II. He was a wealth of information, but he had a rather dry personality and monotone voice and talked in great detail about historical events. Jason, who had just turned four, grew impatient, and during the man's lecture, my son shouted, "Blah, blah, blah!" We were mortified.

"Jason!" I admonished in a hushed tone. "Don't be rude."

The tour guide was very nice about the comment and waved

it off. Even so, my husband and I were still upset and embarrassed. Yet, when I thought about it, I realized we all said "blah, blah, blah" on occasions when we were describing what someone else told us and didn't want to fill in every word. Jason had evidently overheard it and copied it, as any kid his age would do. However, he didn't know where and when to use such a phrase and when it would be considered impolite.

I've often had to tell all my sons that they can't treat others the way they tease and fight among themselves. Billy and David had always received excellent conduct grades on their report cards, even though they could often be loud and rambunctious at home. They knew and respected the line between public behavior and private behavior.

Jason, evidently, didn't recognize that same line. So Kevin, ever the instigator and solver of our kids' misbehavior, decided to take the "get tough" approach with Jason and threatened him with a stint in military school, though he had no real intention of ever carrying out the threat (at least that's what he told me). Kevin even sent away for brochures that were mailed to the house, so Jason would think we were actually considering shipping him off. I was torn between the two of them; Kevin kept saying his "scare tactics" were working and that I should support him, and then Jason would cling to me, crying and saying, "Please don't send me to military school, Mommy."

About two weeks after the last complaint from the preschool teacher, Kevin dropped his threat of military school. I guess he was satisfied with the impact he thought he had made on Jason. David, Jason, and I went to the local Christmas parade soon afterward and sat on a curb to watch all the bands and floats. As a high school ROTC unit marched down the street, carrying rifles over their shoulders, Jason stared at the boys, his eyes getting bigger by the second. Then he turned to me, a little panicked, and asked, "Mom, is that the military school Dad wants to send me to?"

I hid a smile and said, "I don't know if that's the same one or not."

When the next ROTC unit came along, he said, "There sure are a lot of boys who have been bad."

I'd told Jason's teachers that I would continue to talk to Jason about name-calling, but I also informed them that at my house it was like trying to row a boat against a raging river of testosterone. I wasn't sure my efforts would be productive; it was only natural for Jason to copy a lot of what he heard at home. One night one of the teachers called me about scheduling Jason's annual conference, and the name-calling issue came up briefly. During the middle of our conversation, I had to excuse myself a moment to call Kevin into the room. Billy and David both needed rides to different places in the next fifteen minutes, and we had to coordinate our plans. I put my hand over the phone receiver and said to Kevin, "Since you're taking David, you need to take Jason, too, because Billy's meeting will last longer."

Kevin replied in a loud, booming voice, "Okay, I'll take the twerp."

There I was on the phone in the midst of talking to Jason's teacher about his problematic name-calling, and his own dad calls him a "twerp" loud enough for the teacher to hear. I hoped she could now see what I was up against. If I were to stop Jason from using these words, I would have to revamp the dynamics of my entire household. And the manners makeover would have to start with my husband, meaning no more nicknames and no high-fiving after loud burps.

My husband has nicknames for each of us. He calls me "Boss" or "Sir," which is definitely a misnomer; Billy is "Girlfriend" just to irritate him; David has been dubbed "Pumpkin" for reasons I can't even remember, and Jason is "Twerp" to one and all. The other Scouts in David's troop even called Jason this. And yet I was supposed to tell Jason that silly name-calling was unacceptable.

Repeating Kevin's other phrases also has proven to be a problem with Jason. My older boys have to get up at 5:45 a.m. to get to school, and, naturally, they don't like having to get up so early. Once, when Billy and David were lying in bed and complaining about getting up, Jason, whom we thought was sound asleep, shouted groggily from his room, "Life sucks and then you die." He obviously had been listening a bit too well when Kevin replied to Billy's protests about mowing the grass.

That *Super Nanny* program crossed my mind for about two seconds, and I thought about submitting my family's name for a visit from her. But I decided against it. I could just hear her remark in her British accent to millions of viewers: "Undoubtedly, the O'Donnell family has proven to be the most difficult challenge of my professional nanny career." Then an entire argument between Kevin and me would be captured on tape, Billy and David would get into a fight and exchange punches, and dear, sweet little Jason would cuss out the camera crew. No, submitting our family for a reality TV show was definitely a bad idea.

But, I ask you, how is a mom supposed to mold boys into dignified, sensitive young men with a dad like Kevin as their main role model? I love my husband, but he'd be the first to admit he's rather uncouth at times. Our sons learn impolite habits from him I don't even know they're picking up until it's too late. When David was three, he went to a speech therapy class. One of the words he couldn't pronounce correctly was "girl;" he pronounced it "gril." So his teacher was trying to get him to say the word spontaneously, not just repeat it. She held up a Barbie doll of some sort and asked, "What's this, David?"

David looked up and replied nonchalantly, "Hot babe."

The therapist laughed so hard she just about fell out of her chair. I'd been observing the class, so I was right there in the room with them. My face turned bright red. I knew David had picked up that phrase from his father's rendition of Bing Crosby's "White Christmas," which he'd been singing to the boys each morning during the holiday season that had just passed. Kevin's version went like this: "I'm dreaming of a blonde hot babe…"

Could I possibly live in a more chauvinistic home?

If one of the guys whimpers about something like having to do chores, Kevin will tell him to "put some pants on." I know this politically incorrect comment stereotypes women as being overemotional and weak, and I hate to hear it, especially when it comes out of Jason's mouth during Sunday school. I was actually teaching the lesson one week with another woman, who was very prim and proper. She had only one toddler-aged son, and she obviously wasn't conditioned to testosterone-inspired language as I was. A little boy in the class had started crying, and Jason remarked to the woman, "When I do that, my dad says, 'Put some pants on.'" The poor woman's face turned as white as chalk, and for a moment I thought she might pass out. Jason laughed as he said this, not realizing its poor taste.

Luckily, Jason's teachers appreciated his sense of humor, even though they had to discipline him about name-calling. They would share stories with me about some of the amusing comments he made. When they had sloppy joes at lunch for the first time, Jason opened the bun, stared at the red glob of meat and sauce, and told the teacher, "Miss Ellen, this is just sick and wrong." They later dubbed him "unpredictable," which is a good description of Jason.

Still, I felt that all three of my boys could use a manners class, so I began looking for one (too bad there wasn't an adult seminar for Kevin). My older boys didn't call anybody names except each other, but their table manners, eye contact, and skills at introducing people certainly needed some work. My problem with this was twofold: first, making the guys go to manners classes without complaining until my ears were ready to drop off and, second, fitting the classes into their busy sports and Scouts schedules.

Cotillion is the granddaddy of all manners classes, culminating in a three-course meal and ballroom dancing. As much as I'd love to dance with my sons at their graduation from the class, I just couldn't visualize them making it that long. I was afraid just mentioning the idea of them attending this class would send them into a permanent catatonic state.

The less demanding manners courses seemed more feasible, so I looked into those. I signed Jason and David up for a manners class that would teach Jason to be polite in social situations and work on David's table manners and speaking with adults. They also needed practice in saying "Excuse me" because I was sure this would come up many, many times in their lives.

Billy got lucky and didn't have to go to a manners course since the only one offered for his age group was cotillion. However, we still use it as a threat.

"Does that manners class cover hygiene stuff?" Billy asked, as David and Jason were getting ready for their first session. "That's what David needs."

"Come on, Bill, stop teasing," I told him.

"Mom, I mean it. He needs a class that teaches him to take showers every now and then and not to bite his toenails."

"I think I can say beyond a shadow of a doubt toenail biting won't be covered," I said. But actually, hygiene would be a worthy addition to a manners for boys class. Basic stuff like taking showers regularly and using deodorant. David came inside dripping with sweat one day after playing three games of basketball at the gym. "Hit the showers," I commanded, as he walked by me. I had to rear back to get away from his stench. He stopped and looked at me, dumbfounded. "But I just took one this morning," he protested. And in his mind that explanation made perfect sense.

My boys use deodorant, but I have to remind them to do this repeatedly (this is how the word "nag" came into existence, though if we didn't do the reminding, most of the men in America would smell like New York City cab drivers). Having learned from his older brothers, even Jason realizes the importance of smelling decent. When he'd just turned five, I had to take him with me on a stop by the home of an acquaintance I didn't know very well. I was dropping off a box of canned goods for some volunteer work I was doing. Jason went in with me, and after I had talked with the woman for a few minutes, he stated that he had to go to the bathroom. *Oh no, not now, I thought.* "You can wait, can't you, Jason?" I asked in my best "sweet mom" voice.

He shook his head and started wiggling his legs like he really had to go. The woman laughed and said, "Oh, he can go right in here." She opened the door to the hall bathroom, and Jason hurried in. She and I had more chit-chat as we waited for him. Seconds dragged into minutes, and I'm sure both of us were wondering what he was doing in there. Our conversation became strained.

Finally, I went to check on him. I walked down the hall and opened the bathroom door. There he was standing in front of their mirror rubbing on the woman's deodorant. When he saw me, he quickly pulled his shirt back down, set the deodorant stick on the sink, and put his hands in his pockets, trying to look innocent. I jammed the cap back on the deodorant and grabbed him by his shoulders, pushing him out of the bathroom. I whispered, "Just wait 'til I get you in the car." I never explained to the woman what he'd been doing because I was just too embarrassed. I hoped she wouldn't argue about it with her husband later that night. *Damn it, Larry, I keep telling you to put the deodorant back in the cabinet when you're done.*

I also have one final request concerning the "manners for boys" class curriculum: teach them that under no circumstances is the use of whoopee cushions or other gas-simulating devices funny or harmless. Placed in the wrong person's chair at the wrong time, the results can be quite devastating—Aunt Martha still hasn't recovered. The modern, high-tech replacement of the whoopee cushion is the infamous Fart Machine (no, I'm not making this up), which produces fart noises by pressing a remote control. This cute, little item was a gift from Kevin's friend, Chuck. (Oops—forgot to write a thank-you note for that one!) All of my boys thought it was the funniest thing ever. They'd laugh so hard their faces turned red, and they would make snorting sounds, trying to catch their breaths.

With all the snorting, burping, and name-calling, I realize the improvement in manners is going to take a while. But despite some setbacks, Jason has shown signs of promise here and there. At his preschool spring musical program, he stood on stage beside a girl with ponytails that stuck out at odd angles, sometimes blocking out his face and sometimes threatening to poke him in the eye. Jason looked irritated at her a couple of times, but showed unusual restraint and didn't push her off the stage or call her an idiot.

I was so proud.

✦ "You Look Fine"

WHENEVER I PUT on something dressier than jeans, my sons automatically ask me if I have a meeting. They assume since I look halfway decent, instead of my normal stained-sweatshirt self, that I must be headed out somewhere, and "somewhere" in the life of a mom often involves a meeting. And let me tell you, it's pretty sad when a rare night out means the PTA.

Billy and David are old enough now that I don't have to worry about getting a sitter for them. But when all the boys were under age ten, it was always a challenge for me to get away. On those nights, whether I had a meeting or dinner with friends, I just wanted to get ready without having to juggle intervening in the kids' squabbles and explaining homework assignments while cooking dinner at the same time. And adding to my stress, if I needed to be somewhere at 7:00 and had arranged for Kevin to take care of the boys, he wouldn't arrive home from work until 6:50. This meant I had to sprint out the door as soon as he walked in. You've heard of tag-team wrestling, where one guy tags the hand of his teammate, and they switch turns in the ring? Well, we were perfecting tag-team parenting. I'd slap Kevin's hand on my way out as an imaginary bell sounded in my head, and then it became his turn to grapple with the Fearless Flying O'Donnell Brothers.

Just once, I wish Kevin would have come home in time for me to go upstairs and spend ten minutes alone to spruce myself up a bit, so I didn't look like a complete mess. You know, time to put on a clean shirt, refresh my makeup, brush my hair, pee.

I also needed a few minutes to give instructions before I headed out. Essential stuff I knew my husband would have no clue about. "The chicken's in the oven, potatoes in the microwave, salad's in the fridge. You need to go over Billy's math with him because he has a quiz tomorrow and make sure David takes a shower because sometimes he says he has but he hasn't. Jason gets one teaspoon of medicine in the white bottle before he goes to bed and also rub on his eczema cream." You get the idea. A little time to hand over the reins, pass the baton—tag out.

Being rushed and stressed is no way to set the tone for the night and a 100 percent effective way to start a marital argument.

Even though the guys are older now, going out for the night still presents some problems in our house of males. Before I walk out the door, I'd hope my husband and sons would tell me if I needed to make a quick adjustment and that they'd notice the major things like an incorrectly buttoned blouse or wearing two different styles of shoes. In my haste, just about anything can happen. But my guys provide no help at all, seemingly oblivious to my appearance. Haven't I done them this favor for their entire lives, suggesting alternatives to wearing ketchup-spattered shirts or white socks with dress pants to Sunday school? Either they honestly don't notice anything wrong with my clothes, or they don't care whether I humiliate myself in public. Frustrating beyond belief either way.

I'm so weary of leaving the house after standing right in front of them, only to have some stranger point out that my slip is three inches below my dress or my shirt's on inside out or there's a glob of makeup on the side of my face. There was one occasion where I was heading to a meeting, and just before I got out of the car, I glanced in the rearview mirror for one last check. A huge smear of mascara streaked from the corner of my right eye down my cheek, which none of the guys had pointed out to me before leaving. I looked like the lost member of the band Kiss or Tammy Faye Baker after a good cry. However, none of the boys thought it important enough to tell me.

Too bad I can't say this was an isolated incident.

Once, when I was teaching a writing class, a girl raised her hand to tell me I had a tag on my shirt. I looked down to see the long adhesive tag on my newly purchased shirt, with "XL" written repeatedly all the way down it's length (this wouldn't have been nearly so embarrassing if the shirt had been a medium). Had my husband not noticed the long strip of glistening plastic when he said goodbye to me that morning?

Instead of pointing out these things, my husband utters those infamous words that men have been uttering for generations: "You look fine." I don't mean, "You look *fine*, baby, uhhm-mm-mmm," said with a wink. Not sexy fox "fine." This kind of "you look fine" is spit out in a universally understood, bored monotone that conveys the fact that the man actually has no idea what you look like because he has not really looked at you at all. He's merely heard you ask, "Do I look okay?" To which he replies, while reading the sports page or the Dow Jones numbers or taking a nap on the couch, "You look fine."

Then I usually have to find Billy and ask him if my outfit looks okay. At least he bothers to shift attention from his video game and glance at me for a millisecond before he responds.

"You look fine, Mom," he says and shrugs with indifference. He's been trained well by his dad. I sigh, remembering the days of living with two older sisters and my mother, who wouldn't hesitate to tell me if something didn't look right. I recalled the days in my college dorm when my roommates and I always gave each other bits of fashion advice before we headed out for the evening.

But now I was on my own. I had to accept the truth—Kevin and the boys really didn't care what I wore. Yet how could I expect them to when they didn't even care about their own appearances when they went out? Pants too tight, colors that don't match, wrinkled shirts. When I point things like that out to them in an effort to help, they get irritated, whereas most women would be grateful. The only time in our entire marriage that I remember Kevin giving me helpful advice about my clothes was when we were in the Swiss Alps at beautiful Mount Titless, and I was trying on souvenir

T-shirts. As I held one up in front of me, Kevin cleared his throat. "Ah, Sharon," he said, "I don't think you'd want to wear a shirt with Mount Titless written on it." Damn if he didn't have a point. But that's the only time he's ever sincerely been concerned with clothes at all; otherwise, he's seemingly unaffected by fashion faux pas.

Kevin even had his own "left-on tag" incident, though he wasn't nearly as embarrassed as I had been. It happened a few years ago at a large Thanksgiving gathering on my father's side of the family. My dad was one of twelve children, so multiply that by a few generations, and you get the idea of just how crowded the place was. I was sitting with one of my couple of dozen cousins when her young daughter raced into the room yelling, "There's a man walking around with a tag hanging under his arm!" Remembering the brown suede jacket I'd recently bought Kevin, I knew instantly who the man was.

Sure enough, when he came into the room, a huge white tag dangled from beneath Kevin's right arm, and making things worse, I'd gotten it on sale at K-Mart, so that big, unmistakable *K* was hard to miss. When we pointed it out to Kevin, he simply yanked off the tag, saying, "Oh well." It didn't bother him at all that he'd been walking among a houseful of my relatives with a tag advertising K-Mart hanging from his body. I hadn't been with him at the time, so my only saving grace was that in an extended family as big as ours, perhaps no one knew whose husband he was.

Since my guys never seem to care about their attire or help me with mine, I've decided the next time one of them walks out the door with their pants unzipped, which happens quite often, I will not say a word. And then later when they ask me, "Why didn't you tell me my fly was open?" I'll act surprised and say, "Oh was it? I didn't notice. Besides, you look fine."

✦ And in This Corner, Weighing in at Thirty-Eight Pounds...

ARGUMENTS ARE A given in a household of boys. I'm not talking about disagreements or squabbles but loud, rambunctious, physical arguments. These fights reached their crescendo in our home a few years ago when Jason was still small enough to jump on someone's back and hold on like a bull-rider in a rodeo. It added another dimension to his attack. I recall one particular fight back then that occurred while I was trying to finish my weekly column before a rapidly approaching deadline.

"Give it back!" David, who was nine, yelled from the family room.

This demand was followed by some scuffling and pushing noises and three-year-old Jason screaming, "I had it first!" More scuffling. They were probably rolling around on the floor, fighting over a soccer ball or the TV remote, grabbing each other by the neck or the leg. I could picture the scenario all too well, play by play. I sat at my computer trying to work and wondering how long it would take until somebody—or something—got hurt. Earplugs. I needed earplugs to tune out all the screams, whines, and accusations.

Usually the impromptu wrestling matches that erupted in our family room every day didn't last long, although there were about twenty such matches per day. I was so used to the commotion that the noise turned into something akin to background music for me.

"Owww!" David yelled again. "Get off my back!" Jason laughed loudly, doing his best Joker imitation from *Batman*. He obviously had gained the upper hand on his older brother. He had this move where he would run full speed toward his target—this usually being one of his two brothers—and then jump on them from behind, wrapping his fingers tightly around the target's neck. He'd ambushed me a few times, too.

Then there was a loud thud as Jason evidently had a little help getting off David's back. Jason started crying, and I heard the familiar footsteps clomping on the hardwood as he came running into the study to show me the latest injury. He ran in, mumbling something unintelligible through his tears and holding his left arm out to me.

I took Jason on my lap, touched his arm gently, moved it back and forth. No broken bones. I patted him on the back, hugged him, and kissed his forehead. "You're all right," I said. Then I yelled to David, "You guys better behave!" (Yes, the brilliance of my disciplinary techniques astounds me, too. I'm sure Dr. Spock and all those other "how to raise a child" book authors would frown upon my lackadaisical response, but hey, I was working, and I had a deadline to meet.)

After I comforted Jason for another minute, he hopped down and ran back into the family room, growling and probably making a beeline for David again. Going back for more, despite the pain. This is one of the laws of malehood that I'd noticed over the years. Ho-hum. I sighed, hit "save" on the computer and strode into the family room with what I hoped looked like determination.

"Guys, somebody is going to get hurt!" I yelled. "Stop it now." I lunged for Jason but missed. "Do you want to go to your rooms?" I put my hand on my hip for effect. I was really trying to make an impression. They turned and looked at me and shook their heads. I watched as they made a convincing truce and settled down to watch *Rugrats*.

I returned to the computer for a few minutes, only to hear Billy's hoof beats as he galloped down the stairs two at a time. I braced myself; with all three of them downstairs within a square yard of each other, something was bound to explode.

I was right. Before I could type another word, I heard a ball bouncing, a precursor to one of their infamous indoor soccer games. "No playing ball in the house!" I shouted, thinking of all the picture frames and the decorator plate that had bitten the dust in the past year. (Regular items on my shopping list are milk, bread, chicken nuggets, and Super Glue.)

So instead of playing ball, they decided to see who would have the honor of simply holding the soccer ball while they watched TV, an ancient ritual of men that dates back to their cave-dwelling ancestors and how they fought for the possession of rocks. The thought process goes something like this: He got it. Me don't want it. But he got it. So me gonna take it from him anyway.

More scuffling, pushing, and thuds ensued. Then Jason yelled, "Billy hurt David!" as he ran the well-worn path into the study to tell on his brothers. David was whimpering in the family room.

Soon Billy came in and defended himself. "He was messing with me first. Tell him to stop pushing the soccer ball in my face."

David's crying got louder as he entered the study. "Is there any blood?" I asked, continuing to type. This was one criterion on which I based the seriousness of claimed injuries. I didn't mean to sound insensitive, but there'd been too many times over the years the guys would "cry wolf" just to get my attention or get somebody else in trouble. Once David actually bit himself on the arm and blamed Billy for it. We almost had to send out for dental records to clear the whole thing up.

"No," David whined, "there's no blood, but—"

"Then get over it," I said. My husband would tell them this, and it worked, but I never sound gruff enough for it to be sufficiently ominous. "And you guys knock it off," I added. "I've had it!" In any event, things finally quieted down, and I made my deadline with about three minutes to spare.

The injury by which I judge all roughhousing ailments is one Billy received when he was in the first grade. He busted his lip open and dripped blood everywhere one day when David pushed him into a dining room chair. The trip to the emergency room was a long one, with me in the waiting room holding a wet rag on Billy's bloodied, swollen lips. This was our first foray into the world of stitches. We've had other trips to the emergency room, but oddly none of those were caused by roughhousing, rather by things like landing wrong at the bottom of a kiddie slide, resulting in a broken arm for David, or tripping over a crayon box, when Jason almost lost a tooth. I guess that's why I've relaxed a bit about the roughhousing. The worst stuff usually happens in the most innocent situations.

Whenever all three of my boys are in the same room, I get this powerful urge to do my Howard Cosell impression: "And in this corner, weighing in at thirty-eight pounds..." Most often they like to roughhouse in the family room, in which case I retreat to another room to find some peace and leave my husband to referee the boys. The most desperate action I've ever taken to get away was when I spent two hours in the bathroom claiming to have an upset stomach while I was really reading *People* magazine and giving myself a facial. If only I could fake Irritable Bowel Syndrome until all the boys moved out of the house, I might have some time for real luxury and relaxation.

Though I hate to admit it, even roughhousing has its character-building benefits. When David was ten and Jason four, they were cavorting one morning before David left for school, having a good time playing. I took that opportunity to run upstairs and brush my hair, a basic part of grooming that moms sometimes have to forego, particularly in the mornings.

Suddenly, I heard a great crash from downstairs. Then silence. They were obviously dreaming up an excuse.

"What broke?" I asked, stomping down the stairs. It was the kitchen table, the round, wooden kind with a huge pedestal base in the middle. Only the table was now broken off the pedestal, lying on the floor. Jason, who had the tendency to hop on the table when pretending to be Spiderman swinging on a web, blamed David. David didn't deny he had played a role, but he argued that Jason had pushed him onto the table. (This table, by the way, is not the kind you get at Ethan Allen; we got it at one of those warehouse stores that have going-out-of-business sales every week but, miraculously, never go out of business. Point is, it wasn't the Rock of Gibraltar of tables.)

Since Jason seemed extremely energetic that morning and I'd never known David to climb on the table, I—playing judge and jury like moms are forced to do—chose to believe David.

I explained to Jason that he needed to calm down, that pushing David was wrong. Then I popped him on his bottom a few times and sent him to his room. He broke out in tears but did what I told him, crying the entire time.

The rest of the day went by peacefully since the oldest two were at school. I heard the front door slam when David finally came home and the thud of his backpack as he dropped it on the kitchen floor. His feet hurried down the hallway, taking the stairs two at a time. That wasn't his usual afternoon routine; most days he came in slowly, fixed a snack, and sat down to start his homework. Something exciting must have happened, I told myself. News he wanted to share. Maybe an A on a test or a new friend he'd made.

I left the bedroom I was cleaning and went to the top of the steps. I looked down at David, who was about four steps away from me. He stopped when he saw me, a look of fear on his face. "I need to tell you something," he said. My heart sank.

"This morning," he said. I waited, not breathing. "This morning, Jason didn't push me. It was my fault. I was playing with him and lost my balance and fell on the table."

I breathed again, then smiled. "That's been bothering you all day, hasn't it?"

He nodded, his bottom lip quivering. I hugged him, told him he and Jason should not have been so rough, but that I was glad he'd told me the truth.

More than that, I was *relieved* he'd told me the truth. A few minutes later, I went to my bedroom, closed the door, and screamed, "Yes! He does have a conscience!"

✦ Got Balls?

WITH FOUR GUYS living under the same roof, our household almost always revolves around a single, mildly worshipped subject: sports. It's balls, balls, balls, and more balls (with a few pucks thrown in). "What time is baseball practice, Mom?" "Did you get the snacks for my basketball game?" "We can't go anywhere before six o'clock—the Panthers have a game this afternoon." "I know you wanted to go to that play tonight, honey, but I just got some great tickets to the hockey game instead!"

I'll never forget the day I came home to find my decorator plates missing from the wall, replaced by a huge framed poster of Fenway Park with the words, *The Chapel*, below it. We eventually compromised on a smaller, more tasteful photo of the Red Sox's baseball park and put it on our "sports wall:" the wall in our family room where I tolerate the hanging of sports banners and pennants.

I've learned the hard way, in the trenches, that sports will change your life. Even merely watching sports can have an impact on your lifestyle. Because we're avid Red Sox fans, we always buy the Major League Baseball Extra Innings package, which means most nights the TV in the family room is tuned in to a baseball game. Despite being a self-proclaimed sports fan, I still get tired of watching the games night after night.

Watching sports with her three boys is even tougher for my sister, Gail, who fakes an interest in basketball and football just to have something to talk to her sons about. If she had given birth to a little girl in addition to her sons, she would've happily gone to dance lessons every weekend for the past fifteen years. Luckily for me, I've always liked sports, while the thought of dance lessons terrifies me. I can discuss double plays, third-down conversions, power plays, and full court presses as well as any guy, but still, sometimes, I grow weary of constant television sports.

So does Jason. Whenever he's watching one of his favorite non-sports shows, he has a habit of taking the remote with him to the bathroom, so his brothers can't switch the channel. This is the old "sports versus cartoons" debate. Sometimes Jason even hides the remote and then forgets what he did with it, sending us all on an impromptu scavenger hunt. Our whole family watches way too much television, especially ESPN, MLB Extra Innings, Nickelodean, the Cartoon Network, and for Kevin, the military and history channels. But, quite frankly, the TV is sometimes the only thing that helps me retain my sanity. Ironically, at David's school one year, I was the PTA chairperson of Turn Off the TV Week. That's sort of like Tom Cruise being named man of the year by *Psychology Today*.

When my boys and Kevin are in different locations while one of their favorite teams is playing, they call whoever is watching the game and don't even offer a "Hello" or "Hi, it's me"—they say "Score," and the person watching reports the score. Then they hang up. End of conversation. No goodbyes, no "We'll be home in a little while." Nothing. Drives me crazy.

In the spring of 2006, I was with the boys at their dentist appointments (it's a small miracle that all three can be accommodated at the same time) when the receptionist came out and told me I had a call at the front desk. She said it was my husband. My heart started pounding. I worried that something had happened to my parents or other loved ones. I picked up the phone. "What's wrong?" I asked.

Kevin replied, "Tell the guys the Red Sox won in the bottom of the ninth. Mark Loretta hit a walk-off home run."

I paused a moment, looking at the three women behind the counter, who were all staring at me in concern. Then I said, "You called here just to tell me that?" I apologized to the women for the inconvenience. They were really nice about it and laughed, but I couldn't believe Kevin had tracked me down at the dentist's office to relay sports scores. "Couldn't get through on your cell phone," he explained before I hung up. Sharing game scores is the personal mission of every guy, and they will stop at nothing to deliver the news.

Yet, it's not *watching* sports that transforms your household so much as when the boys start *playing* sports themselves. Then you might as well say goodbye to the meager social life you've managed to maintain up until then. You won't have a free weekend until the last one's out of the house working or in college. And prepare yourself for smelly jerseys and uniforms spilling from laundry hampers and jockstraps suspended like decorative elements from various doorknobs throughout the house.

I have to admit, Kevin and I both enjoy watching our sons compete in sports, but still, it's quite a commitment to attend all the practices and games. Writing all these on our kitchen calendar is also a feat within itself. Our typical weekend might involve three basketball games, a baseball game, a soccer clinic, and practice for various other sports. It gets really hard to remember which game is where and when, and Kevin and I have both driven to the wrong gym a time or two. Oops.

Going from one event to another often involves more strategic planning than a military attack. "Okay, I'll take Billy to his

AAU game at nine, and you take David to his baseball game at ten along with Jason. Then after that I'll meet y'all at the fire station for the Scout field trip and drop off Billy there. David's Scout shirt's in your car. I'll take Jason from you and take him to his friend's birthday party, then meet all of you at Jason's soccer match later. Then we can all go to Billy's city league game at 3:30. After that, I'll take the other two home, while you take David to the batting cages for his baseball practice." Then we synchronize our watches and make sure we have directions to all the places before we go our separate ways.

The key here is to make sure you have a can of deodorant and some anti-bacterial wipes in the car, so the boys can clean up a little between activities. This becomes not so much an option, but a necessity as they get older. As a mom who is considerate of people both outside and inside my family, I don't want my sons' body odor to become the topic of conversation after they finish a basketball game and have to rush to another public function immediately afterward. Now, my two older boys have reached the age where they find it humorous to try to hug me or lean their sweaty heads on me right after a game. Thanks, boys, this is the reason I went through labor.

When we go to Billy's basketball games, Kevin always yells from the bleachers things like, "Get tough, Bill!" or "Box out!" or "Get aggressive!" Kevin's voice is deep and carries quite well, and Billy doesn't always appreciate the whole crowd hearing his father's advice. I'm not too comfortable with it, either.

"Shhh," I'll say to Kevin, grabbing his sleeve. (I've noticed other women having to do the same thing to their husbands from time to time.)

"I'm just telling him what he needs to do," he says.

"Yes, I know, but you're so *loud*," I whisper, with a fake smile on my face so the other parents won't think we're arguing.

The thing is, usually Billy will ignore Kevin's comments anyway or maybe turn with a frown and a quick "Will you please stop?" stare. Parents know the stares I'm talking about. But sometimes I can't help yelling things, too, like "Cross the lane, Bill," or "Take it up strong!" but my voice doesn't boom all through the gym like his dad's.

Predictably, Kevin's comments to Billy never went unnoticed by Jason. Soon after Jason's fourth birthday, he watched Billy play and began to shout his own directions. "Play like a man, Billy!" he screamed. "Box out like I do, Billy!" And the laughter he drew from the stands only encouraged him.

Sometimes it gets rough under the boards when boys ages fourteen to sixteen are out there, pushing and shoving for position. I'm amazed at some of the biceps on these guys; it's like they've been drinking protein shakes and bench-pressing since they were seven. At fourteen, Billy was six foot three and still growing, but he hadn't hit the weight room yet. I think it would have been a bit weird for him to do it any earlier; I didn't want my twelve-year-old worrying about how many pounds he could squat, but rather to just be a kid and have fun.

But from my experience, there's nothing as nerve-wracking in sports as being the mom of the pitcher on the mound in baseball. The guy with it all on his shoulders. Everyone watches his every move and sometimes they comment—everything from compliments to criticism. When I go to the games that David's pitching, I like being there to support him, but I'm probably more nervous than he is. My good friend's son, Cal, is older than David and also a pitcher. I used to hear her talk about how she'd get so uptight while he was out on the mound, and I was always glad David played shortstop. Then, when he was ten, David told us he wanted to pitch.

"Are you sure, David?" I asked him nervously. "You're a really good shortstop." I was hoping I could change his mind. Didn't work. And so I became a pitcher's mom, too. He's come a long way from that little boy who ran the wrong way around the bases after his first hit playing league baseball. It was a home run, and he just kept running clockwise around the bases.

So far Jason has played basketball and soccer, but not T-ball because it would be hard for him to adjust to the style of play. I'd shudder to think of his reaction when he found out he'd have to hit the ball off a tee instead of having someone pitch to him. He'd been hitting brother-thrown pitches since he was two and would be totally bored hitting it from a tee. This is all a part of what I call LittleBrotheritis, an ailment that afflicts young boys who have big brothers, making them think they are as old as their brothers and can do anything their brothers do.

The first time this became obvious to us was when Billy and David were playing in basketball leagues, and all Jason wanted to do was run out onto the court to play himself. As a toddler, he didn't understand why his brothers could run up and down on the court but he couldn't. Then the same thing happened with baseball. For Kevin and myself, long gone were the days of actually watching our older sons compete in athletic events; with Jason, our time was instead spent trying to keep him off the field or the court by distracting him with coloring books or Skittles. Eventually, whenever Kevin took one older son to an event and I took the other someplace else, we started drawing straws to see who had to take Jason along.

"You take him!"

"No, no, I took him last time." Love him lots, but he was a handful.

Jason shoots hoops in the driveway with his brothers and has grown up around the sound of a basketball being dribbled on the pavement. Once at halftime of one of the guys' league games, three-year-old Jason was running under the basket and saw a ball coming toward him. He kept running, but he covered his head with his hands as he ran. An old pro at protecting himself. By the time he was four, he'd been hit in the head with basketballs bouncing off the rim hundreds of times (personally, I think this could be the underlying cause of Attention Deficit Hyperactivity Disorder).

When Jason was five, he took a basketball skills class at the YMCA. While all the other kids hadn't a clue what to do, Jason bent his knees, put his arms out, and started guarding the child with the ball. Perfect defensive position. Other moms smiled and asked if he had taken this class before. "No," I replied, "he just plays with his older brothers."

In that same class, Jason reached out quickly and stole the ball from another boy, who immediately burst into tears, prompting his mother and the instructor to rush over to comfort him. Jason turned and looked at me, surprised, with his arms out and palms face-up. "What?" he asked, perplexed. "That's what the other team does."

And he was right. That *is* what the other team does. Just not in kiddie basketball. But due to Jason's case of LittleBrotheritis, he saw no difference in the competitive level of the preschoolers' game and his brothers' AAU games.

Jason is just embarking on his journey through the wonderful world of youth sports. As he learns the rules of the games, he is also becoming more interested in watching college and pro sports on TV and in person. This means our third boy will carry on the cycle of life as usual in the O'Donnell household, where the change of seasons is marked by sports. No winter, spring, summer, and autumn for us—just basketball, hockey, baseball, and football. Yep, there are definitely too many balls in our house.

✦ Temper, Temper

MALES ARE KNOWN to become angry more quickly than females. Or maybe it's just that when they do get mad, they're a lot louder than women and more dramatic about it, making their tempers so much more noticeable. We've had some all-out brawls in the family room at my house, arguments over silly things that quickly escalate to pushing and hitting. The male temper is alive and well and unfortunately has taken up permanent residence in my home. From my husband's aggressive "no nonsense" voice to Jason's furious squeals, getting mad for guys means being loud and ostentatious. Many times I've had to remind them that "the windows are open, guys." I'm sure our neighbors have listened in on many disputes, whether they wanted to or not.

A considerable part of this display of temper has to do with the kind of language the guys have learned to use in both normal conversations and angry outbursts. I've made every attempt possible to keep some of these slang terms from infiltrating my home, but it's been to no avail; after all, I'm outnumbered. With my first two sons, we never used the word "butt." Instead, we politely said "bottom," the word I suggested. "Sit on your bottom," I'd say in my once politically correct house. However, sometime after that third son, it became apparent that *butts* were gradually sneaking into our sons' vocabulary—every day, *butts* bouncing off the walls and more *butts* echoing down the hall. What had happened to my sweet children? Suddenly, it was "I'm gonna kick your *butt*," or "Move your *butt*, idiot," or just a simple "*butt*head."

And we had a similar problem with that infamous word *fart*. For years, I got away with telling my oldest two it was called "passing gas," and so that's what Billy and David called it, too. They honestly weren't aware of any crude variations. I don't remember exactly when *fart* became acceptable in our household; I tried my best to fight it, I promise, but I was just too weak. As parents have said for years, you have to pick your battles with your kids, and I decided this one wasn't the most important.

Also, up until the third son, no one in our home ever dared utter the phrase "shut up." We always asked one another "to be quiet." Always. Somehow that one slipped in after the third son, too. It was as if I had let my guard down with David and Billy, having to concentrate on changing Jason's diapers and breastfeeding, and when I turned around again, there were some new vocabulary words being flung around in the house. Of course, when kids cartoons utter "shut up" routinely, the taboo nature of the words wears off.

"Nuts" and "balls" also fall into the category of words that the older two boys discovered—and I'm not talking about pine nuts or basketballs. This evolved as they began to play and watch sports. I guess it's kind of difficult to use athletic cups without picking up those words. Plus, there's been many a football or basketball game on TV when a player would get hit and double over in pain, and my husband would remark to the boys, "Aw, man, he got wracked in the nuts." Then all of them would stare at the TV, wincing as if they, too, shared in the pain. That's the one time guys show empathy for one another.

I don't do well with the word "nuts." I know how sacred it is to males, and so I'm uncomfortable when I have to use it, even to refer to a food item. I'll always remember one trip to the grocery when I couldn't find bags of pecan pieces, so I absentmindedly said to the clerk, a young man stacking cans of baked beans on the shelf, "Excuse me, where are your nuts?" He stared at me for a moment like I was a pervert until he realized I was actually inquiring about produce.

"Oh yeah, six. Aisle six," he answered, his face turning as red as the can of beans in his hand.

Then there is that awful word *friggin'*, or its derivatives, *frickin'* or *freakin'* or any variation thereof. I was told a long time ago that these words mean the same as the other *f* word, so I've made sure to personally stay away from them. (And don't ya just hate that the *f* word sounds so close to *truck* when little boys are learning to talk?) I began to hear *friggin'* crop up in the conversations of mostly angry people of all ages, seemingly from toddlers on up to grandmothers. Still, I kept to my vow for my family to avoid its usage. Then one day when David was in first grade, his class was going to sing Christmas carols at a local nursing home. He came home the day before the performance and wanted me to listen to him practice the songs. "We Wish You a Merry Christmas" was rolling right along until he hit the verse about the pudding. His innocent voice took a sharp, demanding turn: "Now bring us some friggin' pudding, now bring us some friggin' pudding."

"No, no, no," I interrupted. "It's *figgy* pudding. Figgy, figgy, *figgy*." I guess figs weren't a very common fruit in the minds of first graders—maybe if they were a type of nut, he would have understood. He told me everyone in class was singing the song that way. So the next day he told his classmates they'd been singing the wrong word. Good thing I stopped that rendition of a holiday favorite. I could just imagine the senior citizens shocked by the filthy language of a cherubic choir of first graders.

And there's yet another word that I, at one time, could confidently tell you my sons would never say. That word is *sucks*. I really detest this word that has wedged its insidious way into the everyday language of society, especially with our young people. My sons first picked it up when they attended hockey games where irate fans yelled in unison, "Ref, you suck!" One time I offered an alternative. "Guys," I said, "Why don't we yell, 'Ref, you stink!'"

Billy glanced at me and rolled his eyes (the first of many times to come). "That just doesn't have the same effect, Mom."

The summer Jason turned four, we were vacationing in York, Maine, where we were playing a game of miniature golf. Like his brothers, Jason was pretty athletic, and usually games came easily to him. He was excited about playing golf. But as one putt after another rolled in the wrong direction or veered off into the water, his frustration grew. Finally, one of his putts seemed to be going straight in the hole, but instead, it slowed and rolled back down the incline. Jason could take no more. He jumped up and down, swinging his club in the air, and yelled with all the passion in his being, "This game *sucks!*"

We were embarrassed but had to stifle grins at the sight of a preschooler ranting and raving about golf. All around us grown men stared at our son and chuckled in appreciation, perhaps relieved that their true feelings about the game had finally been spoken; someone so young could get away with yelling what they'd felt on the golf course many times themselves. From the mouths of babes, indeed.

Sure, using certain words is definitely a big part of the male temper displaying itself. And then there is the almost daily physical exhibition of anger. As a mom, I'm always playing ref in the middle of my sons' fights. In our house, the arguing will get so bad and so annoying, I swear you'll feel the urge to pull on a striped shirt and hang a whistle around your neck.

I've given up on the idea of having a coffee table because too much fighting in the name of brotherhood erupts in our family room. When my eldest son was little and learning to crawl and walk, I found out it wasn't a good idea to keep a table in the middle of the room. He knocked his head on it a few times, so I put it in storage in my mother's basement.

Now, as the years have gone by, I've thought longingly of my coffee table. I considered putting it back in place, but I'm sure it would just become an accident waiting to happen, another object for Jason to jump from. I gaze at those family room pictures in the "beautiful homes" magazines—or, heck, even Rooms to Go ads in the Sunday newspaper—and I drool over the family room arrangements with pristine cherry wood coffee tables sitting in front of a stain-free Victorian couch. However, such a gorgeous living area is not meant for me. Sometimes our place doesn't even resemble civilization. Every week, there's either chocolate pudding smeared on the walls, popcorn kernels all over the carpet, or empty Gatorade bottles lined up in front of the fireplace. Guys' décor.

My guys are always blaming each other for something. Usually it involves a video game, chores, or who ate the last of the Cheetos. You know, those really important issues. Sometimes it's teasing that simply gets out of control, which regularly involves my husband, the *adult*, my supposed partner in raising these children. If not for his graying hair and his facial stubble, it would be difficult to distinguish the kids from the parent.

One afternoon, when all of us were together watching TV and reading the Sunday paper, Kevin decided to pull David's pants down below his knees. David shrieked and karate-kicked at my husband, who caught David's foot in mid-air and flipped him over. "Cut it out, guys," I told them. I'd seen teeth knocked out resulting from play just like that. David pulled his pants back up, and Kevin promptly gave him a wedgie. Very mature. Billy laughed and pointed at David, inciting even more anger in David. So David lunged after Billy, while Jason jumped on David's back. Then Kevin tickled Jason, who pulled David's hair. "Guys!" I yelled again. "Billy, David, Jason, Kevin!"

"He did it!" Kevin shouted, pointing at David.

Now I ask you, should I have to discipline my own husband? In a household of boys, the answer is an emphatic yes. Being surrounded by so many of their own gender brings out their innate sense of fighting to survive. "Oh, but they're bonding," some people might say. Perhaps this is male bonding. But what the hell is the female in the household supposed to do while this all goes on? I'm considering producing a reality show where one woman must live in a room with four males as they "bond together" and see how long it takes for her to go absolutely bonkers. Honest to goodness, if I hear Jason threaten, "You want a piece of me?" one more time, it's a one-way ticket to loony bin for me.

3

Woe, A Woman's Work is Never Done

— Sure Signs You're a Mom of Boys —

+ Nobody replaces the toilet paper roll except you.

+ You're always out of ketchup and milk.

+ Power Ranger parts are stuck in your vacuum cleaner.

+ Your most dreaded chore is not cleaning toilets; it's cleaning the floor *around* the toilets.

+ Your greatest sense of accomplishment comes when all the dirty clothes hampers in the house are empty at the same time.

+ Balls of wadded-up socks litter your entire house.

+ You used to shave your legs every day, but now it takes an Act of Congress.

+ The money you spend at the grocery store rivals the national debt.

+ The TV remote is treated like The Holy Grail.

✦ Drowning in Laundry

I came home from a church meeting one night and found my family room floor covered with laundry. "What the heck happened in here?" I asked Kevin, who was on the couch reading the newspaper.

"Jason folded the laundry for you," he said, looking up from the paper for about a millisecond.

"Why'd he do that?" I asked.

"I wanted him to earn some money, so he'll appreciate it more. I gave him two bucks to fold laundry."

I looked around at the mess, the mismatched socks, the haphazardly "folded" towels, the shirts rolled up in balls. "I'll tell you what," I said, "next time I'll give him two dollars just to let me do it." We exchanged glances. I paused, mulling over the sanity of what I'd just said.

Sure it was a good idea to teach Jason the value of a dollar, but, please, let's not do it at my expense. It would take me longer to re-sort the laundry that Jason had done than if I had folded it in the first place. I made a mental note to pay Jason to wax my husband's car just so I could see the look on Kevin's face when he viewed the finished product.

As anyone with children knows, doing laundry is one of those things that has to be done on a regular basis or the result can be overwhelming. It accumulates so rapidly that I've watched piles of clothes build from the size of mere ant-hills to giant sand dunes in a span of hours. I once sent a new mother a card that read, "Parenthood is like laundry..." Then you opened it up and it read, "a never-ending job." It's one of those chores that can be the most frustrating because it's never finished. But everybody expects you to know where every item of clothing is and have it waiting for them whenever they need it. Nothing is more irritating than when it's time to leave for one of my son's games and he yells from upstairs, "Hey Mom, where's my jersey?" Had it not occurred to him until the last possible moment that he would need this jersey?

Unfortunately, we don't have a laundry room; our washer and dryer are situated upstairs at the top of the stairs behind some bifold doors. Thus, this narrow area at the top of the steps has become our makeshift laundry room. And since I'm always behind on laundry, when the boys' friends come over to play, we're continually saying, "Just step over the clothes at the top of the stairs." And nobody wants to even attempt to tackle the sock pile. All those boy socks look alike, differing only slightly by size. I have no idea whose is whose, so the sock pile sits in the corner of the hallway, a permanent fixture in our home. Quite honestly, though, I'm not sure what our dog, Fenway, would do without the accumulation of dried laundry loads at the top of the steps. He burrows down in the clean clothes and makes a comfy little nest for himself. If I ever get a chance to catch up on laundry duty, Fenway will be very disoriented, searching everywhere in vain for his favorite place to nap.

Yes, I realize clothes become wrinkled when left to sit in a pile after being washed, but I can only get to them so many times during a day. At least they're clean, save for a little dog hair. Our family just goes through far too many clothes in a day for this process to run smoothly. Besides, usually I take out the things that wrinkle easily and drape them over the banister until the guys hang them in their closets. I've discovered that the bar of an Abdominal Roller exercise machine also makes a terrific place to drape unironed clothes. Not what it was intended for, but at least I'm getting some use out of it.

I've also become wiser over the past few years and have started dropping off Kevin's dress shirts at the dry cleaners. When we were first married, I ironed his dress shirts every day because I looked at it as one of my new responsibilities. I even gained a certain pride from a well-ironed shirt, believe it or not. During these same newlywed years, I used to hang freshly ironed clothes on the washer/dryer closet door in our little apartment. I remember once when my mother-in-law was coming over, my husband started taking down the hangers of crisply pressed shirts to put them in his closet. "No, don't do that," I'd told him. "I want them to stay out so your mother can see how well I'm ironing your shirts."

No joke, I actually said that. I was a sick, sick person. I've always despised ironing, as a matter of fact, but back then I guess I was trying to be the perfect wife. Now I know better. Ironing is the most time-consuming, frustrating, monotonous task there is. My mother, bless her heart, knows how much I detest this chore, and whenever she has some free time, she'll call me up and say, "Bring some of your clothes over if you want me to iron them."

"I'll be right there," was always my reply, regardless of what I happened to be doing at the time.

I'm not sure my beloved husband fully appreciates the enormity of the laundry responsibilities in our house. Last summer I came across an e-mail he'd sent to a fellow Boy Scout leader, asking about getting a second Scout Leader shirt for himself. To explain his need for one, he wrote—and I quote—"The laundry cycle here at the house does not always run on a weekly basis."

What!? Excuse me? Not run on a weekly basis? It runs on a *daily* basis, I'll have you know, but with laundry piling on top of more laundry, the stuff that starts out at the bottom sometimes stays at the bottom. I can't help it if my boys' dirty underwear multiplies faster than bunny rabbits on Viagra. And, listen, if you're missing your all-important, special red Scout shirt, by all means, dive in the hamper, find it and put it on top of the pile. Perhaps then the item will finally get put into the washer by your devoted, exhausted wife—whom you vowed to love and cherish, by the way—and then your precious red shirt will be folded and waiting for you just as you've come to expect during the last eighteen years of marital bliss. Well, the honeymoon's about over, sweetheart. It's time you jumped in and swam a few laps in the laundry yourself.

Aside from the inordinate stacks of laundry, when the males in my house work out at the gym or play sports a lot, they bring back clothes of the most offensive odor. These workout clothes usually smell so bad that Kevin and the boys wrap them all in a towel and leave the bundle on top of the washer, so it'll get first priority, like a surprise gift waiting for me to unwrap. When they do this, it puts me behind by an entire load of laundry. If that cycle were to keep up, I'd never get any of my own clothes washed. My suggestion is for someone to start a gym that has its own laundromat where guys can wash their own stinky clothes before coming home. Gymolaundry. I'd buy stock in it.

Then there's the "olfactory conflict;" ironically, women have a much stronger sense of smell than men. It's a cruel, little joke—men sweating so much and women blessed with a very strong sense of smell. I can't walk within ten feet of a hockey equipment bag that's been zipped up for three days. Phew!

I'm getting better at drawing boundaries in the laundry game. Kevin asked me a few years ago with a dreamy, faraway look in his eyes, "Remember when you used to put my clothes in my drawer after you folded them?" I nodded and handed him his stack of folded laundry to put away himself. The honeymoon's over, indeed. But I will say Kevin and the older boys do help out sometimes; Billy actually does a pretty good job of it. Kevin gets the job done, but he doesn't take the time to make sure socks match up correctly or to place them in the appropriate boy's pile of clothes. They can always tell when Dad has been on laundry duty.

The whole process is so badly mixed up that Jason will take out a pair of pajamas from his drawer, hold them up, and exclaim with an ear-to-ear grin, "Hey, these match!" Finding matching pajama parts shouldn't create such joy in a preschooler. Lately, though, I've been neglecting the laundry. Instead of folding a pile of clothes for each guy, I simply throw each item in the direction of the appropriate bedroom. I figure somebody will pick it up sooner or later—knowing my guys, probably later. But all the laundry will eventually get done. I just have to make sure Kevin doesn't hire Jason to do it anymore.

✦ Potty Training 101

The pressure was on. There was only a month and a half to go before Jason, at age three, started preschool and had to be completely potty trained. The preschool at our church where he would be going has a rule that children beginning the program have to be out of diapers and pull-ups. I barely remembered potty training my other two boys and didn't recall the potty training "deadline" looming over us like this with Billy and David. If I stopped and dwelled on the possible repercussions, pure panic set in. In order to attend the school two mornings a week, Jason had to be consistent with his, shall we say, bathroom habits—not just pretty good most of the time. Talk about incentive. Nothing like the dangling carrot of having two free mornings a week to get a mother moving.

If a child who starts this particular preschool in the three-year-old class has repeated bathroom "accidents," then the child loses his or her spot in the class, and the next kid on the waiting list is able to take the vacated spot. Though the pressure on these children and their parents can be a bit overwhelming and ridiculous, I'd still hate to be the mom of the first child on the waiting list, wishing some poor kid would wet his pants at school.

Of course, a lot of kids have the occasional accident, but at least my older boys had them at home, not at preschool. Schools always ask that parents send in a change of clothes "just in case." I remember those days of driving to pick up Billy and David, hoping that when I saw them they would still have on the clothes they dressed in that morning. "Please, let him still have on his Elmo shirt and Big Bird jeans," I'd say to myself, casting a nervous glance toward the sidewalk where they lined up.

So with Jason due in preschool and somewhat lacking in bathroom independence, our house suddenly became Potty Training Central with a single mission: code name, Operation Flying Dry. This process consumed the entire household, even changed our lifestyle. Sadly, I admit that for a month and a half I derived my self-worth from the toilet habits of a toddler.

First, we changed the surroundings of our work: There were new boxes of flushable wipes, cushioned kid-sized seats that fit the toilet, a colorful potty chair that played musical interludes after a successful attempt, training videotapes from the 1970s that encouraged toddlers by praising the potty adventures of other kids, an assortment of children's books to read in the bathroom, and that most revered rite of potty training passage—the sticker chart. Our sticker chart was posted right outside the downstairs bathroom, complete with Power Rangers, Buzz Lightyear, and Dragon Tales stickers.

The chart concept was simple—Jason got to choose and put up a sticker every time he used the potty. It was slow going at first since he fought all my attempts to stop his playtime to go take care of business. Finally, I gave him a sticker for simply standing near the potty chair without screaming. This bit of reward psychology worked, and soon he began to use the small musical potty chair. The problem was that with my older two boys I had been able to plan my schedule around their potty training, but with Jason, just when we were making progress, I'd have to go to one of the boys' baseball or basketball games or school events. We eventually saw some progress, though.

Of course, there were those people on talk shows who said things like, "Well, my little Johnny was trained at thirteen months. It took me only one day." Or, "My Sarah *wanted* to do it. She came to me and took me by my hand and led me to the bathroom." Comments like these are very discouraging to frustrated parents of normal toddlers. So are books with titles such as *Potty Train While Teaching Your Toddler Spanish* or *Dr. Bill's Positive Potty Training with a Smile* (even though his wife probably handled all the dirty work with their kids). Instead, I think all of us mortals could relate much better to such books as *Potty Training for Dummies and Parents Who Have Lost All Possible Enthusiasm* and *Triathalons, Climbing Everest, Potty Training, and Other Life Challenges.*

There's a Dr. Seuss book called *Oh, the Places You'll Go.* That title, I imagine, might have been inspired by potty training because Jason certainly elected to "go" in many different places. There was the time when he yelled out, "Mommy, I'm going to the bathroom," as he was hiding between the wall and couch. I had to lean over the back of the couch and pull him out by his arms before too much damage was done. There was also the time in the car when I was running late to a doctor's appointment. I had to pull over to the side of the road, grab our portable potty, get Jason out of his car seat, and position my bewildered child on it before he started to "go."

Instead of saying, "Mommy, I have to poop," he used to say, "Mommy, I'm pooping." He was a lover of stating things in the present tense, even though the "action" was yet to happen. His remark, though grammatically incorrect, always managed to get a quick reaction from me— I would drop any activity and rush to scoop him up in my arms (at arm's length of course) and carry him to the bathroom. Sometimes I didn't even know where he was in the house at the time he called out one of his alerts, which is a definite no-no in the potty training manuals. Once I was upstairs folding laundry when I heard him call from somewhere downstairs in an angelic voice, "I'm pooping." Down the stairs I ran, barefoot and leaping over action figure toys strewn hazardously in my path. I whipped around the banister, sprinted down the hallway, slid across the freshly waxed kitchen floor, flung myself over the top of the leather couch and landed in a standing position, out-of-breath, searching frantically for the culprit. Surely this will be an Olympic event someday. Though it turned out to be an exercise in futility, the old saying, "better safe than sorry," certainly applies to potty training. Believe me, there have been numerous times when I've been sorry and had to run to the store for carpet cleaner. The one time you chose to ignore him would be the time you lived to regret it.

At the time I was potty training Jason, my older boys liked to call things we did together as a group "family activities;" potty training, strangely enough, fell into that category. Nothing but potty training can reduce an otherwise sane, educated (I use these terms loosely) family to standing around the toilet cheering and applauding the youngest son's latest achievement with the enthusiasm of a Broadway ovation. If the happy event took place when Billy's and David's friends were over, they would stare at us open-mouthed, their eyes darting around for the nearest escape route. And so it happened that other family members could no longer answer nature's call without Jason applauding each of us, telling us what a "good boy" we were.

Jason soon graduated to the big potty, more commonly known as a regular toilet, lacking the bells and whistles. He even got up there himself and began to ask me to leave. "I want you to go out," he told me, in his most serious tone. My toddler was growing up, beginning to value independence and privacy.

Of course, Kevin saw Jason's success and remarked, "But he needs to stand up like a guy, not sit down." Everybody's a critic. (He also worries about Fenway the dog not hiking up his leg when peeing, so there may be some kind of obsession involved.) My response was simply, "I got him to this point. Now it's your turn."

I knew from my experience with the other boys that soon after potty training was complete, Jason and I would face what I call The Great Bathroom Dilemma. This is the point when a young boy doesn't want to use the women's room any more, making it difficult for his mom when she and the boy are on their own in a public setting. Case in point: when David was three and a half—a good eight months past his potty training completion—he and I went shopping at the mall. Soon after we got there, David told me he had to use the bathroom. When I tried to take him into the women's bathroom with me, he pushed me away, saying, "I'm a big boy." Yet, he was scared to go into the men's room by himself, and I was leery of that myself.

But the boy had to go, and I had shopping to do. I was finally able to drag him into the women's room while he screamed, but he refused to use it, grabbing the stall door with his hands and pulling away with all his strength. After I'd pried his fingers from the door one by one, he still refused to use the bathroom, so I decided to call his bluff and leave, certain he would then change his mind. But he didn't. He followed me into the hallway where he promptly threw himself on the floor and refused to leave the hallway between the two bathrooms. Solution? We went home immediately without the blue Icee we had agreed upon if he behaved well.

Potty training is certainly a challenge—one usually left to the lady of the house, not the dad. But if she's the mom of a boy, eventually she'll reap her reward: that wonderful time when he's too old to go the ladies' room, so Dad has to take him to the men's restroom, which then leaves mom with five convenient minutes to eat or shop in peace. See ya later, boys.

✦ Midnight Grocery Shopping

I HATE IT when I find myself at the grocery store after eleven o'clock at night hunting for about a hundred items that I didn't want to take the time to find earlier in the afternoon with the boys in tow. These late-night excursions usually occur several times a year, but the last time one of these happened, I experienced a rude awakening. Just as I made it down the last aisle, I turned the corner and discovered that the only cashier lane open after eleven o'clock was self-service, or in my case, snail-service.

My cart skidded to a halt, sending cans toppling and vegetables rolling. After a half hour of carefully selecting products and searching in vain for those little packs of crackers with spreadable cheese, I didn't feel up to playing cashier. Several people stood in line to scan their own items with the "user-friendly" computer. There was a man with beer and cereal; a young woman, probably single, with the latest issue of *Cosmo*, a frozen pizza, yogurt, and shampoo; and another man with a carton of milk, orange juice, and a box of Krispy Kremes.

And then there was me. My cart was so full I could barely see over the top. It would take until Hawaii freezes over to find all the barcodes on each of the items and scan them individually. What was the store manager thinking? It's almost midnight, and I'm grocery shopping; do they think it's been a *good* day?

I contemplated pushing my cart into a far corner and running out, but my conscience wouldn't let me do it. Besides, I'd have to come back the next day and find the same items all over again.

Most late-night shoppers dash in for a few crucial items, so scanning them is no big deal, but I wish the grocery stores would take a little pity on us late-nighters with cartloads. Finally, I took a deep breath, resigned to spending the next twenty minutes of my life doing something a trained employee could take care of in five.

I had entered a few items already when a high school-aged guy with a store name tag walked by. His name was Danny. I caught his eye with my best forlorn face and a loud sigh, an instinct that years of motherhood has taught me. "Could I help you with something, ma'am?" he asked.

"When did y'all change to only self-service after eleven o'clock?"

"We implemented that a few months ago," he replied, smiling proudly, as though the idea had been a medical breakthrough.

"Do you see how many items I have?" (We moms haven't seen the "12 Items or Less" lane since our first contraction. I dream about it sometimes.)

"Let me help you, ma'am." Danny jumped into action, steering my cart to the self-service line. And he did his best. He helped me scan the items and re-scan some stubborn ones. He punched in three-digit numbers for my plastic bags of fresh produce and weighed each one; unfortunately, I had most of the Garden of Eden with me: apples, oranges, bananas, strawberries, and some veggies, too. Finally, after more than ten minutes, Danny and I were done with the groceries. And I was utterly exhausted.

When I got home after midnight, Kevin, was sitting on the couch watching a *JAG* rerun. I dropped the grocery bags on the counter a little harder than usual to let him know I had made it back. He muted the TV.

"What's wrong?" he asked. I didn't answer right away. He stood up quickly and turned to me, fear on his face. "You didn't back into somebody's car again, did you?" he asked.

I waved my hand in dismissal. Then I went on to explain my experience at the grocery store, how tiring and annoying it had been. But after the car question drew a negative response, he was too relieved to have much sympathy. He tried to explain that technology like self-scanners means store employees can be used for other duties during slow hours, thereby making the store more productive, helping to keep prices down, and benefiting the consumer and the overall economy.

Curse the day I married a financial analyst.

I set a can of peaches on the counter with a thud and stared at him. "For this kind of customer sacrifice, they should be able to get us out of the national debt."

"Did you use the coupons?" he asked.

"You've got to be kidding. No way was I going to try to deduct nineteen coupons on that computer myself." Then I jumped into a tirade about my disdain for grocery shopping, housework, and the never-ending chores of parenthood, and ended it all with the refrain we so often repeat in words yet never follow in action: "We really do need to get away."

Kevin nodded. "You could've come with me to Pennsylvania two weeks ago," he said.

I stopped in my back-and-forth trek to the pantry, stacking cans, and gave him my best "Are you crazy?" look. "That was a cremation ceremony for one of your relatives. If we have to start counting stuff like that as our time together, we're in serious trouble."

As I was putting up the last can of green beans, I noticed a note from one of my boys on the counter. "Mom," it read, "I need some raisins, marshmallows, Ziploc bags, and colored toothpicks for a science project tomorrow. Forgot to tell you. Sorry."

I considered having my husband go out for the items, but I came to my senses. He'd never spring for the real Ziploc bags or even locate the toothpicks.

So it was back to the grocery store. Back to the same aggravating, mother-proofed, economically beneficial self-service line.

I sure hoped Danny was still hanging around.

◆ Helping with Homework

HELPING WITH HOMEWORK comes with the territory of being a parent. For those folks who go so far as to home school, my hat is off to you. If I attempted to teach my kids every day, all day, you'd see me on the six o'clock news standing on the window ledge of a tall building. For me, just a couple of hours of homework is challenging enough.

I remember how, as a young girl, my mother and I used to sit together at the kitchen table, and she would patiently call out spelling words to me. Even if I misspelled one we had gone over just before, she didn't lose her cool. My father stepped in when it came to the tougher math courses. Math was always my weakest subject, while it was my father's academic forte. He would try to explain algebra and then glance over to see if any of it had gotten through to me. Usually, he could tell by my sighs and furrowed brow that it hadn't. He'd pause a second and then try another approach, saying, "In other words…" I'm sure he got frustrated with me and had thoughts like, "How in the heck could a mechanical engineer's kid have a brain like this?" But to his credit, he never showed a hint of annoyance.

Contrast these peaceful memories to what goes on at my house. I admit I'm not the most patient person when it comes to helping my sons with their schoolwork. I get irritated at their lack of focus, confused by the teacher's ambiguous instructions, and distracted by all the other things I need to do. And, yes, I sometimes yell. I know about all those parenting experts who say, "If you speak softly, your children will listen to hear what you're saying." Let me hear the experts speak softly when their kid has a math test, a science test, and an art project due the next day, but he's forgotten his science book and notes at school. I hate having to go on the Internet to look up facts about how rocks form. What's really tough is when one of my sons has an assignment and is not given the basic information to work with. I remember David having an assignment in third grade that required answering lots of questions about measuring with the English imperial system and with the metric system. However, they weren't given the information about equivalent measurements.

I was leafing through my cookbooks looking for measurement charts when the phone rang. It was the mother of one of his classmates on the line, sounding as frustrated as I was. "How many tablespoons are in a cup?" she asked frantically.

Neither of us had a clue. Thank God for the Internet. After an hour of learning about meters, grams, yards, cups, liters, and many more terms of measurement, the homework was done. And I was drained. Both children said the teacher had not gone over this info with them first. Did she expect the parents to remember this stuff from their school days? I think there's some sort of statute of limitations on this kind of knowledge, and once we get past a certain age, we get to erase it from our brains (of course, with algebra I never had it grasped in the first place).

Moms are usually the ones who field homework questions, which often become a nightly disaster. I assist my children with all subjects except math; this is where Kevin normally takes over. I've lived my life as a mom in dread, wondering if and when my math genes—or lack thereof—will show up in the boys. (I think my fear of parallel parking stems from my ineptitude at math, too. All that backing up and turning. There's some geometry in there somewhere. Angles and stuff.)

It's sad to think that one of the questions that plagues me most, if anything should ever happen to my husband, is: "Who's gonna help the boys with their math homework?" Sure, there would be other concerns, but this is the one I worry about every weeknight when the homework process cranks up at our house. At least now Billy does his assignments on his own and can—I hope and pray—help his younger brothers in the future (if they can converse without insulting or hitting one another).

I've seen some of those incredible, home-school families on TV news programs. After watching them, I feel unworthy of the title, "Mother." Usually, the family has five or six kids, and they never fight, the mother never yells, the house is spotless, the kids do their daily chores with smiles on their faces, stopping occasionally to hug their siblings, they speak three languages, are two years above grade level, and Mom and Dad hold hands as they stand beside the newly planted vegetable garden in front of their two-story house that they built with their own hands.

Now consider the typical scene at our house: David is lying upside down hanging off the couch with his legs sticking over the top, doing his math homework with a pencil the size of a paperclip. "Sit up!" I scream at him. "You can't do homework like that." Then he grabs a Nerf basketball and turns to shoot it through the plastic goal hanging over the kitchen door. "Two points, baby!" the electronic goal announces, playing a Dick Vitale recording.

"Turn that thing off!" I yell. By this time, Jason is running to get the ball, shouting at David that it's his turn.

"Mom, Jason threw a shoe at me," David says.

Billy sits in front of the TV watching ESPN, eating a bowl of cereal, and studying a vocabulary list. I'm working simultaneously on a PTA project and a column with an impending deadline. The doorbell rings, our dog, Fenway, starts howling, and then I notice the pot of potatoes on the stove is boiling over. Utter chaos. The homework hours are difficult enough at our house; home schooling would be unthinkable.

Of course, I care about my sons' academic success and have been there to help and encourage them. I've bought a whole bookcase of supplementary teaching materials, and I've worked with them the best I can. Heck, I've even ordered *Hooked on*

Phonics videos from those infomercials. Both Billy and David have been good students overall, so we've been lucky. Still, I've noticed some bothersome things along the way.

There have been a lot of studies done about how boys learn differently from girls and that education in our schools is geared more for girls. Boys are generally louder, more physical, and need to move around more, yet schools expect students to be quiet and still. I believe there is some truth to this, but it's not enough of a problem for boys to use it as an excuse for failure. One of the main areas where I've noticed this boy/girl difference in our schools is in the novels they read for class in middle school. David just couldn't get into some of those books, and after I picked one up and started to read, I could see why; it was a "girl's" book with events that girls could relate to much more readily than boys that age. When I tried to explain to David that one of the characters was in love with another character but knew he had to leave her behind, David was unmoved by the poignancy of the story. He got this perplexed look on his face, kind of like the expression Kevin makes whenever he happens to come across the Lifetime Channel. This book was just not guy stuff, and I could see how any male reading it would probably not do very well on the test. I even looked at reviews of the book on the Internet, where I found that girls absolutely loved it, while middle school boys just didn't get it. Of course, I adored the book and was sad that I couldn't discuss the beauty of the writing and the emotions it evoked with my son. Or my husband, for that matter.

David has always liked to read sports-related stories. When he was in fifth grade, a Red Sox player released a biographical book called *Idiot*, which was the name the Red Sox players called themselves the season they won the World Series: They had fun, they kidded around with each other to deal with the stress, they acted like idiots. Knowing David would read sports stories, I bought him a copy of the book. Later on at a teacher-parent conference in the school library, his teacher and I were discussing David's school work while David read at a nearby table. His teacher commented on how intently David was reading, and we both looked over at him. Just then David shifted in his seat, lifting the book up a little so the front cover was in full, unavoidable view. Of course, *IDIOT* was spelled out in huge red letters. I leaned way over to my left to block the teacher's view and launched into some impromptu questions about field trips, hoping she wouldn't notice the title.

I consider myself proficient in language arts, but even I was ready to condemn the English language when David was in elementary school, and the weekly spelling word sorting assignment was due. Saying words out loud repeatedly while trying to determine if they have the "oo" vowel sound or the "u" vowel sound is not a fun way to spend a Monday night. Instead of moving on to the good old "*i* before *e*, except after *c*" rule or when to double the consonant when adding *ing*, David spent three years studying one-syllable words and their vowel sounds. Sometimes I threw in the towel, saying, "Go call Johnny and see what groups he put his words in." It turned out Johnny and his mom had no clue either, and there was just as much screaming going on at their house as there was in ours. Years from now when I think this memory has long since faded, I know I will hear a young mother mutter the words "spelling sorts" as we pass on the sidewalk, and immediately I'll go into wild, inexplicable convulsions, requiring sedation and further medical treatment.

Even homework for preschoolers can be taxing on a mom. Most pre-schools have a letter of the week and teachers tell the kids to bring something that starts with that particular letter *every single day* of the week. This has been medically-proven to cause undue stress in moms. It's okay when the weekly letter is *s* or *d*, but some of the other letters are impossible. When Jason was four, I loathed the arrival of "Letter X Week" and ran totally out of ideas by the fifth day. We'd done "xylophone" and "x-ray" and a few other words I pulled from the dictionary. I couldn't handle the thought of having to come up with yet another "x-object" to take to school. Finally, I decided it just wasn't worth the effort. I looked at Kevin and said, "Oh, hell, let's just let him stay home today."

Projects are another reliable source of stress: Create a board game based on the pioneer westward movement; create a game about integers; select your favorite scene from the book and paint it on poster paper; sculpt a clay bust of the main character's face; make a map of South America using uncooked macaroni noodles. These are just some of the projects my boys and I have coped with over the years. Evidently, some teachers think students are really budding artists, just waiting to have their hidden talent discovered by a middle-aged social studies teacher. When Billy and David were each in fourth grade, they had to make a salt and flour landform map of their home state of North Carolina.* After Billy had done his, I was tempted to keep it in the garage, so when David reached the fourth grade, he could just turn in Billy's. However, as I discovered, salt and flour don't hold up very well after a year.

But helping with homework goes hand in hand with motherhood. Besides, you do recall some things along the way. I mean, how many of us actually remember how to spell *aard-vark* or that there are sixteen tablespoons in a cup?

Note to North Carolina parents of children under age 9: you may want to seriously consider moving to another state before your child reaches fourth grade and gets this traditional "salt and flour map" assignment. Maybe head to Wyoming or Colorado—one of those nice square states. The Outer Banks with their capes jutting out into the sea are beautiful and full of history, but a real pain to build out of wet flour on a piece of plywood. Sculpting this jagged coastline would have been a challenge for Michelangelo.

✦ "I Promise to Love, Honor, and Cook"

I enjoy getting together with family and friends for potluck dinners, I really do. I enjoy the fellowship, but if I have to make one more blankety-blank casserole to take somewhere, I'll unite the women of America, and we'll march over every square foot of our nation's capital. We'll carry signs and chant catchy slogans as we protest every woman's expected role in cooking, particularly at events that should be fun and carefree for everyone (does the phrase "bring a dish to share" ring a bell?). Cooking is a time-consuming job, and somebody in a house of males is always hungry.

A few years ago, when one of my nieces was telling me about a guy she was dating, I made clear the importance of having a partner with culinary talents. "This guy I'm dating is really cute," she told me, smiling, with a dreamy look in her eyes.

"Can he cook?" I asked, glancing over at her.

"He made the dean's list last semester," she said.

"Great, that's great," I remarked, nodding. "But can he *cook?*"

She furrowed her brow and shrugged. "I don't know. He's a terrific soccer player, though."

"Um-hmmm. So if you were on one of those bachelorette game shows where you get to pick a guy, and it came down a handsome, athletic, smart guy or one who was a fabulous chef, you'd take the handsome guy, right?"

"Sure, who wouldn't?" she responded.

I made a noise like a game show buzzer. "Bzzzz. Wrong answer." Then I patted her shoulder, touched by her innocence and naivety—she who was unmarred by years of marriage and innumerable hours spent over the stove. She, who didn't realize the ideal husband was a plastic surgeon who loved to cook and had been to massage school.

"Just wait until after the honeymoon, sweetheart," I told her, "and you'll understand." She'd know soon enough what it was like for the guys to watch football on Thanksgiving while the women bustle around the kitchen. Was this a birthright or something?

It's no coincidence that "cook" happens to be a four-letter word. If I had a lot of time and everyone in our family liked the same dishes, I think cooking might be fun, even creative. As it is, cooking is just one more tedious chore. I know men work, too, and some even help around the house, but eating a good meal cooked by someone else at the end of a long day should be a pleasure for women to enjoy, as well. I know Kevin does the taxes, takes care of the insurance and retirement plans, and works hard at his job. But cooking is a task I must do just about every day, and I get absolutely burned out from it. I must have cooked chicken seventy-five different ways over the years.

Preparing lunches is a lot easier than making dinners. Making lunch for my three sons usually doesn't require a lot of work. Throw some chicken nuggets in the toaster oven, get out some applesauce, open a can of soup, pour some juice. Yet if I leave Kevin at home with the boys during lunchtime, inevitably when I return, the boys are starving. "What did you give them for lunch?" I'll ask my husband.

"They said they weren't hungry," he replies, as he munches on a sandwich. We've discussed over and over how you have to make the lunch even if the boys "say" they're not hungry; they just don't want to stop playing video games long enough to eat. What Kevin also doesn't realize is they're not hungry because they've slipped upstairs with a bag of cookies and a box of Goldfish. Happily, my older boys can now make lunch for themselves, and if they feel like being nice, even help out their little brother.

Now, I try to plan my dinners and often use recipes that I've collected over the years. It's a good thing my mother only lives twelve miles from me. Not only is it great to have a nearby babysitter and confidante, but it's also nice to know it doesn't take a long distance call to ask her a dozen questions about a recipe.

"Hey, Mama, it's me." These quick, in-the-midst-of-cooking phone conversations usually happen while I'm stirring something in a large pot or bowl. "I'm out of baking soda, so can I use baking powder instead?" Or, "My homemade vegetable soup isn't thick enough—what do I do?" My mother is known in her church and community for being a wonderful cook, particularly for her chicken salad, homemade rolls, and coconut and pineapple cakes. She set such a high standard that it's difficult for my two sisters and me to live up to it. So it's no wonder I often pick up the phone, wooden spoon in hand, and dial my parents' number for her advice.

Out of all the dishes I have ventured, meringue intimidates me the most, even with my mother's tips written on an index card. The first time I attempted to make it was when Kevin and I were newlyweds, and he had invited some friends from work over for dinner. I wanted to impress them, and so, recalling the oohs and aahs my mother's piping hot banana pudding always elicited from Sunday dinner guests, I decided to try it.

I had heard all those stories about how tricky it was to make meringue—so tricky, in fact, that even the weather can affect the way it turns out. My mother told me it would be easier simply to buy a box of Cool Whip and put that on top, but I was determined to make the meringue just like she did. I separated my eggs perfectly, added the exact amount of sugar, beat it just right, and it started to get foamy like it was supposed to, though it never turned stiff and formed those characteristic "peaks" that all the cookbooks go on about.

Later that afternoon while I was out, my mother called to see how things were going with the dinner preparations. Kevin, who had been glued to a Red Sox game on TV, answered the phone and was, of course, oblivious to my trials and tribulations. "How'd the meringue turn out?" asked my mom.

"I don't know," he said, "but there are three bowls of white stuff on the counter, and she's gone to the store to get some Cool Whip." I'm sure my mother knew then it wasn't going well.

A few years ago, my mom gave each of her three daughters one of those recipe card books, complete with each of her recipes written in her own handwriting. I knew it must have taken her a long time to write each recipe three times. "Why didn't you just use a copier?" I asked when she delivered them to me.

She shrugged. "I didn't mind writing them out."

"Okay," I said absentmindedly, still thinking how much faster it would have been to make photocopies.

But over the years, as I've flipped through the recipe book, I am so glad she took the time to write them instead of using a copier. I'm comforted by the sight of my mother's distinctive handwriting, as familiar to me as my own. Written by the same hand that had written gym class excuses for me growing up and signed, "We love you, Grandson," on birthday cards for all my boys. She had painstakingly and precisely written all the ingredients, all the preparation hints, trying to anticipate any questions we might have, so that perhaps years from now when she's not around for us to call any more, she'll still give us the answers.

Cooking is one of life's necessities; however, I wish it wasn't always necessary for *me* to be the cook in our home. Every mom knows the awful feeling of spending $200 at the grocery store only to still have nothing good to make for dinner. There always seem to be plenty of snack foods, house cleaning products, and toothpaste, but nothing that really makes a hearty meal.

And these days there are so many things to consider when cooking for one's family: Is it nutritious? Low in fat? Low in cholesterol? Taste good? Does it have preservatives? Is the meat fresh? Can you prepare it and have it ready to eat in between one son's basketball game and the other's Scout meeting?

When Billy was about five, I remember sitting at the kitchen with him and some of his friends when they started singing, "Take Me Out to the Ball Game." I joined in but the lyrics came out uncontrollably: "Take me out to a restaurant, take me out of this house!"

Men don't like to go to restaurants as much as women, and the real reasons have nothing to do with the cost of a meal. More than men, women can truly appreciate the pleasure of being waited on. "Would you care for ground pepper on your salad, ma'am?" "Butter on your potato?" "Let me clear that plate out of the way." Ah, heaven.

Another reason is that women want to eat a variety of food that actually tastes good. Men just eat to get full. That's not to say they don't enjoy a flavorful steak now and then, but when they get hungry, they're simply looking to fill their bellies. Women don't do this. Therefore, it's logical that we females like to get together to go out and eat, to try the new restaurant in town.

My advice? The next time they ask, "What's for dinner?" hand them a Domino's coupon on your way out the door to meet the girls at a bistro. Every "cook" needs a night off once in a while.

✦ Bringing Home the Bacon

Although my husband has always been a good provider for our family and has shared everything with me, I've had a difficult time thinking of our checking account and savings as "our" money since I'm not the main bread winner, by far. Society gives us all the impression that if it's not *paid* work, it's not important work. I know that's not true, but I sometimes still feel guilty about spending money since I don't contribute a lot financially.

Even buying a gift for my husband can be tough because I think, "He made this money, so how can I buy him a 'gift' when it's his money to begin with?" I know that's faulty reasoning, but I want to be honest about how we mothers can sometimes feel. Often, I look back on a writing job with the state tourism department I was offered when Billy was four months old. Perhaps I should have taken it. At the time, though, Billy was my priority, and I couldn't imagine leaving him all day.

So I became a stay-at-home mom, even though there's not an awful lot of staying at home that goes on in my life. But when you take away the paycheck, the lunches with colleagues, and the sense of accomplishment derived from a job, there's a lot of one's typical self-worth taken away also. Sure, I've spent a lot of quality time with the boys, and I've done countless hours of volunteer work for the PTA, my church, the March of Dimes, the American Red Cross, and other organizations. Yet, I still feel my worth and my value are defined by society in dollar signs. That's one of the reasons I started to do some part-time work, teaching writing in schools and also working out of the house doing public relations jobs.

The most difficult part of being a "working mom" is having less time for my sons' school-related events. When David was in the first grade, I was disappointed that I couldn't go on his first field trip of the year to a local zoo. He asked me a number of times if I could go, and I felt guilty telling him that I couldn't. The day of the field trip was during my first week of teaching writing, so when I arrived home that afternoon, I was stressed out and exhausted. It wasn't until dinner that David looked shyly at me and said, "Mom, you forgot to ask me something."

"What did I forget?" I asked, baffled.

"You forgot to ask how my field trip was," he said, his big blue eyes gazing into mine. My heart sank. I felt terrible. Perhaps a little thing to most people, but to me it was huge. It was in that instant that I realized the disadvantages of being a working mom. My son's big field trip had slipped my mind. And he knew it.

Working out of the house has been no picnic, either. Since faxes and e-mail have become so widely used, America's workforce has changed, with a lot more people working from their homes. For most people this arrangement works well 95 percent of the time; however, I've found that, as the mother of three sons, it can sometimes be quite challenging. With writing deadlines to meet, phone calls to make, and kids to watch over, it seems like I'm constantly juggling domestic and professional matters.

When I first went back to work part-time, Jason was three months old and not a napper by any stretch of the imagination. Fifteen-minute catnaps throughout the day, and he was ready to go. Hearing friends talk of their little ones' three and four-hour "naps" was frustrating. They call that a nap? To me, that's hibernation. So I adjusted to working with the sounds of "It's a Small World After All" echoing in my head as Jason lay on a blanket nearby. Sometimes, while holding him in one arm, I would even type on the computer or talk to clients with the phone wedged between my ear and shoulder.

Billy and David were ages nine and six back then, and they helped out by doing chores when they were on vacation from their year-round school. The problem with the older guys and trying to run a business from home came down to one thing: the telephone.

Sometimes I was expecting an important business phone call, and the guys knew not to answer the phone. However, knowing and remembering were two totally different things. So there were times my public relations clients and reporters called the house only to hear a shy six-year-old mumble "hello," while Nintendo provided background music. There should be a routine or system to prevent this from happening, but I never found a solution. My way of dealing with it was, when the phone rang, I'd yell at the top of my lungs, "Don't answer the phone! Don't answer the phone! Do *not* answer that phone!" At the same time, I was grabbing a pen and notepad and jamming a pacifier into the baby's mouth to keep him quiet.

One time Billy and David got into an argument while I was on the phone, and David came to look for me, not realizing I was still talking to a local reporter about an article for a client. I was upstairs, and I could hear David coming up the steps toward me, screaming and crying. "Mom! Billy hit me," he yelled. I raced to my bedroom door, put a finger to my lips, and stared at him sternly, my eyes so wide they were popping out of their sockets. David, still screaming, kept coming down the hall toward me. I pushed the door closed, and it unexpectedly slammed. The bewildered reporter—who has since become a friend and now understands—asked what was going on, at which point I had to level with him. My calm facade exposed.

However, even worse were the days I was potty-training the boys while doing media volunteer work for the bone marrow donor program. While talking to reporters and health organization presidents, I can recall trying to cover up urgent cries of "Gotta poop, Mom!" with a coughing spell. Sometimes I was even helping with, shall we say, the "process," in the bathroom, while holding the phone receiver between my chin and shoulder and spouting out statistical data about bone marrow. I've heard other parents who run businesses out of their homes say they've been in similar situations. Little does the caller know what's really happening on the other end of the line. This is definitely a situation where you don't want one of those new phones with video capability.

Another challenge with me going back to work was how it affected our family's morning routine. As Jason got older and went to preschool, I continued to teach part-time, meaning Kevin was in charge of getting him ready for school. When I'd leave for work most mornings, Jason would still be asleep. One time, I called Kevin on my cell phone with specific instructions for getting Jason ready—what to give him for breakfast, which allergy medicines he needed, what coat to wear, etc. I even reminded him that it was *E* week at school and so Jason had to bring something each day that started with an *E*. "I already put a toy elephant in his backpack," I told him.

I thought I had all the bases covered with Kevin. But later

that day, when I went to pick Jason up from school, he was dressed in a shirt four sizes too big, hanging down around his ankles. I'd thought Kevin could have handled at least the getting dressed part by himself, but apparently I was wrong. He'd put David's shirt on Jason by mistake.

When Jason got to the car, I asked, appalled, "Why didn't you tell Dad that was David's shirt?"

He looked at me and said matter-of-factly, "Mom, Dad doesn't care."

And so the beat goes on.

I admire those women who manage their lives well enough to work full-time. But it's not easy to be a stay-at-home-mom or a mother who works at home, either. Motherhood and womanhood require making sacrifices and trade-offs that most men will never have to contemplate, and so just "bringing home the bacon" should never be the only thing that defines a person's contribution to the family.

4

Thou Hath Vowed For Better, For Worse

— Sure Signs You're a Mom of Boys —

+ You try to use one of those haircut clippers at home and end up giving your son a Mohawk.

+ You consider inventing a "testosterone level" monitor to go along with those carbon monoxide alarms.

+ When you manage to get your sons and husband to attend a play, instead of saying "intermission," they call it "halftime."

+ They only flush when you're in the shower.

+ Your glassware cabinet only contains plastic cups from sporting events.

+ You look forward to going to the dentist just so you can read a magazine and relax in a chair.

+ The most romantic movie you've watched in the past five years was *Die Hard II*.

◆ OPPOSITES ATTRACT?

As THE ONLY female in a household of five, I often find myself lost in a world of sports, bathroom humor, and laundry. It's a rewarding yet challenging experience to live with Kevin and the boys. Forget about men being from Mars and women from Venus—we're not even in the same solar system. Often it seems as though my husband speaks an entirely different language than I do, but there's no pocket dictionary, like the kind I used to have in French class, to flip through and decipher his meaning. Ladies, we're on our own.

The first point of difference, the experts say, is communication styles. Like most couples, I tend to want to open up and talk about things, while my husband keeps to himself. Once, while we were watching a news report in which an American man had met and was marrying a Russian woman who didn't speak much English, I turned to Kevin and asked, "How can he fall in love with someone he can't even communicate with?"

Kevin stared at me blankly and asked, "Huh?"

I shook my head. "Never mind," I mumbled. Instead, I picked up the newspaper and read. Silence has sometimes been easier than trying to attempt a conversation. Over fifteen years of marriage should have taught me there's more to communication than simply speaking the same language. I thought back to that personality test the minister had us take during our pre-marriage counseling, how it showed we were incredibly different, at extreme ends of the scale. Had my brain been totally out to lunch? I should have hopped up from that leather chair in the reverend's office and hightailed it out of there, leaving Kevin and the rev staring at one another.

We were *opposites*, for God's sake. Like hot and cold, summer and winter, talkative and withdrawn, attentive versus oblivious, female and male. That little personality test was a sign, but somehow I missed it or simply refused to see it—the absurdity of two opposites living in peace side by side for the rest of our lives. The plot line of *Rambo* was more believable.

But I didn't run out of that office. I believed in the concept of marriage, even though the very nature of it makes its success a questionable proposition. Somewhere between the concept of marriage and the reality of marriage, though, a lot of things become painfully clear. Opposites are *supposed* to attract like magnets to steel, but in our day-to-day lives we all search for some much-needed compatibility, too. I bought into the romance of it all, dismissing the wisdom of the personality test, dismissing the minister's raised eyebrows. That's probably how most marriages happen. And we are left to discover how the "for better, for worse" vow leaves out something essential: what about all that mediocre stuff in between? The extreme highpoints and low points of one's life are usually easier times for a spouse to show devotion, whereas the stuck-in-the-mud, stressful routine of everyday life is the true challenge.

The things men and women consider important differ, as well. There was one time we were having several couples and their children over for dinner, and I told Kevin I'd need some help cleaning up. And clean up he did. He spent all morning cleaning up the *garage*, for heaven's sake, when our guests would never even set eyes on the inside of the garage. I knew he'd been meaning to get around to organizing it, but why did he have to choose that precise time when doing other things was so much more important?

"Prioritize," I told him, as I've done countless times before. Yet he looked at me with that blank stare again, like the words out of my mouth had been suddenly translated into Swahili. "The garage can wait until later," I explained slowly, emphasizing each syllable, so I could perhaps get through to him. "The inside of the house can't." But it never sunk in.

Common interests are another area where the Mars–Venus thing comes into play. Although I enjoy and understand most spectator sports, I also love to go to plays, book readings, character-based movies, and other artsy kinds of things. Kevin, on the other hand, will find any excuse not to go, or if he does go, he looks at his watch so many times it's embarrassing. As we sit among sophisticated theatergoers waiting for the curtain to rise, he looks impatiently at his watch and asks me, without bothering to lower his deep voice, "What time is kick-off?" Everything is a sports analogy.

The first time I ever got him to attend a play was a memorable night. We had just started dating. As we came out of the theater in silence after a moving rendition of "Bring Him Home" from *Les Miserables*, I waited to hear his response. He said nothing. I'd hoped he would be as moved as I was, so we could talk about our feelings, bringing us closer on another level. He cleared his throat, and my heart leapt, waiting for his opinion of the play.

"*Revenge of the Nerds* comes on TV in an hour," he said. I wasn't sure I'd heard him right. How did we go from an award-winning Broadway play to *Revenge of the Nerds* in 5.2 seconds? Shouldn't there be some sort of transition there? I should have run then, just like I should have in the minister's office, but again, I didn't. And thus I pay the price.

When Billy and David were nine and six, respectively, I decided to take matters into my own hands, to make an effort to keep this male, anti-theater gene from continuing through the generations. I decided to take the boys to see the Broadway on Tour production of *Annie*. Sort of an arts appreciation night. Both of them have quick wits and have at one time or another entertained the idea of acting, so I thought they might like to see other kids their age on stage in a major production. I was a bit concerned, though, the night of the play, when David walked through the doors of the theater and yelled, "Hey, where's the popcorn?" Better, I guess, than bringing my husband along and having him ask, "Hey, where's the beer?"

I stole some glances at them during the first act and was relieved to see they seemed to be enjoying it. At intermission (or, rather "halftime," as their Dad taught them to call it), Billy disappeared to go to the restroom. He still hadn't returned to our seats when the lights dimmed and the curtain went up for the second act. I was all set to go out on a search mission when I spotted him making his way down the aisle. He plopped into his seat, out of breath. I leaned over and whispered, "Where have you been?"

Without taking his eyes from the stage, he mumbled, "Went to call Dad to check the score of the hockey game." My shoulders drooped in disappointment. My arts appreciation night was a failure.

David asked in a loud whisper, "Who's winning?" A few people gave us perturbed looks as if to say, "Why don't you go home and watch *The Simpsons*?"

"Shhh, guys," I scolded them. I sat back in my seat, resigned to the fact that sports would always take precedence over theater in my house and that I might not be able to talk to the boys about another side of them, a deeper side. Oh well, I reminded myself, they are their father's sons. The old saying about the apple not falling too far from the tree certainly applied in this case. So I lost myself in the rest of the show, my soul flying with the spirit of the music.

Later while driving home, I heard singing coming from the back seat, and when I realized it wasn't the *James Bond* theme song or the N.C. State fight song, I just about drove off the road. Billy and David were singing softly, their sweet voices struggling to hit the high notes of "Tomorrow," Annie's theme song. *"When I'm stuck with a day that's gray and lonely, I just stick out my chin and grin and say— ohhh—Tomorrow, tomorrow, I love ya, tomorrow..."* A chill rushed down my spine as I realized the play had touched them. I smiled. My mission had been successful. Someday their wives are going to thank me.

♦ Don't Leave the Shopping to Hubby

There are some things men shouldn't buy at the store. Toilet paper, for example. Off-brand products seem to scream at them: "Buy me! Buy me!" And men often listen, regardless of the product's quality. Toilet paper is one thing you don't skimp on; the cheap versions are usually so rough they could double as sandpaper.

And don't get me started on buy-in-bulk kitchen trash bags with no drawstring. By the time I'm ready to take out the trash, the bag has slipped down in the container, spilling popcorn kernels, melted ice cream, sticky pudding cups, and chicken parts all over the kitchen floor. Even when I ask my husband not to use any more of those bags, somehow they end up lining our trash can. His attitude is that he bought them, and he intends to use them—all five hundred.

Got to be a guy thing. It has become a silent war between us, with me refusing to empty any trash can containing one of those bags. No wonder the divorce rate is so high. I wonder if this "off-brand" thing is what they mean by "irreconcilable differences?"

This is why I do 95 percent of the grocery shopping even though I detest it, especially since we go through food so quickly with our three growing boys. I drive to the grocery store in a month more times than Jeff Gordon drives around the racetrack.

But on those rare occasions that he has to buy the groceries, Kevin shops as if he has forgotten everything he knows about those closest to him. He'll get the strawberry yogurt for me, when he knows (or should know) I've eaten nothing but peach for the past five years, and he still buys the off-brand oatmeal that my boys hate because it's too lumpy, even though he's heard them complain about this very thing lots of times. Then I go out later and buy the right kind, while the cheaper oatmeal sits in the pantry for months, maybe years, gathering dust and my disdain.

And there's his obsession with coupons. When we were first married, Kevin would tape grocery receipts to the refrigerator, showing how much money he'd saved with coupons the few times he shopped for food. He would mark the amount he'd saved with a yellow highlighter and then stand back and admire it like it was the *Mona Lisa*. The man was—and is—a coupon aficionado.

Compare this with *my* shopping philosophy, which holds that every checkout lane is a finish line. No matter where I go, I'm simply trying to get through it as fast as possible.

Shopping has become a lot easier as Jason has gotten older. When he was two, I'd have to give half my attention to him in the store or else he'd throw a temper tantrum. He usually became angry because he wanted to get out of the cart and walk like his brothers or because he had an overwhelming desire to open the new box of graham crackers or grab a banana from the produce section and bang it against anything in his path. He also played a game the purpose of which was to throw out the cans of food when I put them in the cart. This game kept my reflexes sharp as I often had to block or catch cans of Spaghetti-Os before they knocked a fellow shopper unconscious. By the time I'd get to the front of the checkout line, Jason was usually screaming about something, and all I wanted to do was get out of the store. I'd forgotten all about those coupons in my purse and didn't remember them until walking across the parking lot. And then I'd spend the drive home imagining another excuse to explain to my husband why I hadn't used the six coupons he'd given me.

Most men don't understand how to shop from a long list— what I refer to as "real" shopping. I only send Kevin out for simple things like milk and bread because I've learned over the years that even when he goes with a list of very specific items, he always comes home with the wrong stuff.

One time, several years ago, I took a chance and sent him for one out-of-the-ordinary thing. A can of pumpkin. That's all. The next day I was supposed to help the children in Jason's third-grade class make pumpkin pies, and I realized I needed one more can of pumpkin. "Get the pure pumpkin, honey—*not* the pumpkin pie mix," I told Kevin. I even showed him the label on the other can I had. "Look at it," I said, pointing to the words "pure pumpkin." He nodded, and I assumed the message had been conveyed.

About ten minutes later, I heard him come in from the store, set something on the counter, and then go into the family room to check the football scores. I went in the kitchen and looked at the can on the counter: Pumpkin Pie Mix. *Arrrgh!!!*

Shopping for items other than groceries is also a challenge for my husband. Kevin, God love him, doesn't comprehend that shopping involves careful selection, not simply grabbing something off the shelf or hanger. One Christmas, he gave me an extra, extra-large raincoat as one of my gifts, when I wear a medium. I had to roll the sleeves up about two inches just so I could actually use my fingers.

I am in awe of married couples who shop together (this does not include the ones where the husband sits quietly and watches the wife model fifteen different outfits—that's sick). I admire those husbands who seem sincerely interested in finding the right size of jeans for a hard-to-fit teen or the perfect birthday gift for his mother or the coolest costume for his child for Halloween. Kevin has never gone shopping with me for such items, though I would gratefully welcome his input in these decisions.

So whenever I see men shopping with their wives, I can't help but be intrigued and envious. I find myself staring, totally mesmerized. I actually try to catch the man's eyes, so I can peer into them for a moment, expecting to see some sign, some clue, as to how he became a "man shopper." I like those kinds of men, but I've never had the honor of having one in my family. Not my father or brother and certainly not Kevin. There must be a chromosome mutation somewhere that sets apart the rare man shoppers.

None of my sons like to shop, either. They don't care about finding what looks good on them or even great sales (unless it's hardware).

Last year I came across a nice leather jacket for Billy on sale for $14. I could just imagine how handsome he'd be in it, so I bought it. When I got home, Billy complained, "Oh, Mom, I don't want to wear a leather jacket."

"Sometime," I told him, "you're going to need another kind of coat besides those sweatshirt hoodies."

Still, Billy protested. Then Kevin said, "Billy, I'm gonna tell you what my dad told me when my mom brought home stuff: 'Just take it and put it in your closet.'" Billy looked at him, surprised that his dad seemed to be siding with me in a fashion disagreement. Kevin shrugged and explained to him, "It doesn't mean you have to wear it, but it does mean tonight's argument will be over."

There was one time when Kevin actually bought an "imperfect" clothing item that was on sale. We were in a sporting goods store near Boston just after the Red Sox had won the 2004 World Series. Though he bought souvenir T-shirts for the guys, Kevin scoffed at the $20 T-shirt prices and wasn't planning on buying one for himself—until he saw the sale item. It was a dark blue shirt with red letters that read, "Red Sox—hampions, 2004 World Series." Yes, that's "hampions," as in someone made a mistake at the T-shirt factory and left off the C in "Champions." "Hey, this is only five bucks!" Kevin exclaimed, delighted with his discovery. We all glanced over at the shirt he was holding.

"Dad," Billy said stoically, "it says 'hampions.'"

We thought perhaps he hadn't noticed. "Yeah, I know, but it's only five bucks," Kevin said as he put it in our cart.

That's male logic for you.

◆ "What's-Your-Name"

Frequently, when I attempt to call one of my three sons, I'll say the name of the other two before I finally say the right one. And when I do this, they always respond with, "You sound just like Grandma."

If I want to call Billy, I stammer, "David...Jason...Billy," realizing full well that I'm following the same pattern as my own mother with my three siblings and me and even her grandchildren. We know who we're talking to, but the ability to state that person's name aloud temporarily eludes us. Sometimes I give up, saying, "Hey, What's-your-name, come here."

I don't have to run through a list of all my friends' names when I'm about to call one on the phone, but parents say their children's names so often that it becomes routine, increasing the likelihood that such mistakes will be made. Even so, Billy and David like to tease me about using the wrong names. When Jason was three, he'd just grin at my mistake and say, "I'm not David, Mom, I'm Jason." He didn't take joy in pointing out my forgetfulness back then, but he soon joined ranks with the older boys and started making fun of my misnomers.

Billy and David have also mentioned that it's usually me, not

Kevin, who suffers these momentary memory lapses and can't remember our sons' names. And they're right. But I'm at home with them more than their dad is and use their names much more often than he does: "Billy, what did you do with my pile of important papers when you cleaned up the kitchen counter?" Or "David, clean your room and take any cups with milk in them downstairs before they curdle and grow mold." (Not an uncommon incident in our house.) Or "Jason, get down from the top of the stairway banister right now!" By the time I go through such scenarios day in and day out, their names are the least of my worries—I just want to get my point across.

But there was a time Kevin struggled with the name thing, too. However, his mistake wasn't because he slipped up and said the wrong name; he truly didn't *know* the right name.

We were at the emergency room last year after Jason had fallen on gravel outside and cut his hand pretty badly. Stitches were definitely needed, but we had to spend time in the waiting room first. While I comforted a scared Jason on my lap and held gauze to the cut, Kevin filled out the insurance forms. He scribbled something down, paused, and looked over at me.

"What is it?" I asked.

"Jason's middle name is Thomas, right?" he asked.

I stared at him for a moment, disbelief on my face. I shook my head slowly and glanced at the floor.

"It's not Thomas?"

I bit my lip and looked him square in the eyes. "No, it's not," I managed to say, thinking of the months before Jason was born and how we'd had such a hard time deciding on a middle name. Kevin wanted to have the middle name honor an uncle of his named John, but we thought "Jason John" didn't have the smoothest ring to it. Kevin then brought up the topic with his uncle, who said that since he already had a nephew named after him, what he'd really like would be for us to name our baby after his father, Kevin's grandfather, who'd died years earlier. His name had been Thomas Steven, but there was already a Thomas in the family named after him.

So after all this, we decided on Jason Steven. You'd think it would have been memorable enough for Kevin to actually remember. "My gosh," I thought to myself in the waiting room. "It was even *his* relative."

Kevin looked at me blankly. I wanted to make him sit and suffer trying to figure out his son's full name, but the forms had to be completed. I finally helped him out.

"It's Steven," I said, rolling my eyes and sighing. This was one slip-up he'd be explaining for a while.

His eyes brightened with recognition. "Oh yeah," he replied casually, jotting the name down on the form. Then he started writing down all the insurance numbers without needing to look at his insurance card. Astounding. The man could remember multiple eight-digit numbers, but not his son's full name.

I might have to call out each of my children's names before I get the right one, but at least I'm aware of what their names are.

Sounding like my mother may not be so bad after all.

+ A Good Night's Sleep

As any parent knows, once you have a child, you will never, ever sleep well again. This is particularly true of mothers. From the newborn stage to waiting up during the teen years and listening for the sound of their car to insomnia over their escapades away at college, moms keep late night hours.

When Billy was three and David was a baby, I spent a lot of time in the middle of the night going from Billy's room, where he was having night terrors, to David's room, where he wanted to be fed or changed. I remember after one especially tiring evening, I asked Kevin to get up in the morning with Billy, so I could catch a few extra winks. "I was up a lot last night," I mumbled.

"Yeah, I know," Kevin replied, yawning. "I heard you." He sounded annoyed. "I'm exhausted," he said.

I wasn't sure if I understood correctly. I somehow managed to lift my head from the pillow and peered at him through blurry eyes. "You're tired because you *heard* me?" I asked.

"Mm-hmm," he answered, stretching. "The kids sure kept us up." It was something about the use of the pronoun *us* that bothered me.

"Just for the record," I informed him, "if you're going to say the kids kept you up at night, you actually have to get out of the bed in order to make that claim."

Kevin looked at me. "But I woke up all those times you got up," he said.

"Did your feet ever touch the floor?" I asked.

"But I—"

"Did your feet touch the floor?" I asked again.

"No, they didn't," he finally admitted.

"Then it doesn't count. If your feet don't touch the floor, you can't say you were 'up' with the kids." This became one of the slogans of our baby/toddler-raising household along with the proverbial, "You wake him, you take him."

The nighttime routine is also sort of the mom's territory, too, in most houses. Giving the baths, reading the obligatory storytime book and other nightly rituals. Usually I treasure this special time before bed with my boys because this is the time they become my little boys again, no matter how old they are. This is the time they say things that might be bothering them or ask questions that have been on their minds. This is the time Jason still cuddles or the other two want me to scratch their backs.

Sometimes at the end of the day, I think I'm too tired to go through this nighttime routine, yet, when I hear Jason ask, "Mom, will you read me a book?" it's very hard to say no. When the boys were younger, they even slept in our bed sometimes, against the advice, I realize, of practically every parenting expert in America. It became a special treat for them, but in the long run, it ended up being a special treat for Kevin and me. We liked the closeness of the boys, to be able to reach out in the middle of the night and feel their small hands or hear their steady breathing.

When Billy was about two and a half, he was particularly hard to get to lie down at night, always thinking of excuses to delay bedtime. One night I decided to use some psychology on him. Knowing he was a big Mickey Mouse fan, I picked up the stuffed Mickey he slept with every night and pretended that Mickey was saying something to me. I leaned in closer and asked, "What's that, Mickey?" Then I pretended to listen some more. "You're really tired and want to go to sleep?" I handed Mickey back to Billy who cuddled him. I was pretty pleased with my creative parenting.

Then he, too, pretended Mickey was saying something to

him. "What's that Mickey?" Billy asked. There was a pause as he held Mickey closer to his ear. "You want to sleep in Mom and Dad's bed?"

Touché. Outwitted by a two-year-old.

The other thing about nighttime is that it takes a woman much longer to get ready for bed compared with her spouse. Spouse brushes his teeth, strips down to his underwear, maybe pulls on a T-shirt, and plops into bed. Back when I used to have the energy for my own nightly ritual after the kids went to bed, I would annoy Kevin by how long it took me to actually climb into bed. The bathroom light bothered him, as did the noise.

Once when he complained, I stomped out of the bathroom with a jar of eye wrinkle cream in my hand, glaring at him. "After I put my eye cream on, I will proceed to apply stretch mark ointment to my thighs, after which I will put on some age-spot fade cream on my face. Did you know hormones in pregnancy cause age spots? They do. So do birth control pills— damned if we do and damned if we don't."

He stared at me like I'd finally snapped. Perhaps I had. In any event, that was many years ago when I actually had some semblance of control over what I looked like. Now I just fall into bed like he does.

Getting a good night's sleep in our camper is even more of a challenge. The first trip we took after we'd bought it was to Myrtle Beach. It just so happened that the third night we were there, the weather took a turn for the worse, with howling winds and rain. Around ten o'clock, the local weatherman broke into regular programming on the TV, reporting a tornado warning for the area. Not just a watch, mind you, but a warning, meaning one had already been sighted somewhere.

It was in effect until 3 a.m. And there we were in our camper that shook when someone closed the refrigerator door. I did not feel safe.

Apparently, nobody shared my concern because they all fell asleep soon after the warning. I, on the other hand, fought off sleep as I lay in my bed watching the local news filled with weather reports. I couldn't possibly let myself start snoozing when killer winds could strike at any moment. The news anchor even suggested those in mobile homes should consider finding places to stay that were more sturdy. As the wind kicked up again outside, my heart began pounding. I learned a lot about the geographic location of South Carolina counties that night as warnings and watches came and went. If things got worse in our immediate area, I was prepared with a flashlight in hand to wake everybody and get the heck out of there.

Thankfully, the night passed without a tornado touching ground near us. The guys woke refreshed, while I was really dragging. "Why didn't you get any sleep last night?" Kevin asked.

"Because I was waiting up in case I had to save our children's lives," I told him.

"Oh," he said, and picked up the newspaper.

One reason we got the camper was because its sleeping arrangements were easier than having to fit all five of us in two double-sized hotel beds. Sleeping in the camper usually means that I wind up sleeping with Jason on the queen bed, while Kevin and the other boys divvy up the bunk beds and sofa bed. This arrangement worked much better a few years ago when Billy could fit into the sofa bed without much problem; however, when he hit six foot three at age fourteen, it became difficult for him to fit into the bed, not to mention the shower.

On our most recent trip to Disney World, I was reminded again of how tough it is to get a good night's sleep in the camper. This vacation I now refer to—affectionately, of course—as my eight days in a rectangular space with four guys, a dog, and a bathroom the size of a short phone booth. Jason, the poor little fellow, has had eczema since birth, particularly on his hands and legs, so he would often wake up more than once during the night crying because he itched. This would happen more often on vacation because he wouldn't sleep as soundly. Therefore, I'd be up at least twice a night with him, rubbing on his creams and ointments. And to my amazement, Kevin and the other boys always slept right through this.

One night during this trip, Jason, who was five, woke up coughing so much that he actually threw up. After taking care of that situation, he and I went back to bed, only for him to awaken again because his stomach hurt, and he needed to go to the bathroom—badly. *Please, God, don't let everybody get a stomach virus while we're stuck in this camper*, I prayed. Fortunately, it turned out to be just a one-time thing. We fell back asleep again, but about an hour later I heard a loud thump, then screaming, and woke to find Jason had fallen out of the bed onto the floor. I got up and comforted him, again perplexed as to how everybody else was sleeping through all this.

The next morning, the sun streamed into the camper's windows much too early for me. Suddenly, I felt Jason sit up in the bed beside me. I cursed under my breath. "I slept great!" he shouted. I slowly rolled over and gave him a "you've got to be kidding me" look.

"No, you *didn't* sleep great," I told him through clenched teeth. "You threw up, had diarrhea, and fell off the bed." Jason didn't seem fazed at all as he grabbed the TV remote and switched on cartoons. I pulled the pillow over my head, dreaming of I-95 and the road home. Home sweet home in my own bed.

♦ "Me" Time

I'll never forget the time years ago when I came home from a PTA meeting to find my husband, two sons, and my husband's best friend gathered around the TV watching a John Wayne movie. Billy and David, ages seven and four then, watched as The Duke got on a horse and galloped away, tall in the saddle, after just shooting the heck out of the bad guys. "Now that, boys," said my husband's friend who shall remain nameless (even though his name is Chuck), "is a real man." Kevin nodded, adding a philosophical "yep," as he lay back in his recliner.

"Yep," Chuck repeated as the two of them stared off into space, thumbs in their belt loops. Come on, guys. What's next? Tipping imaginary cowboy hats with a "Howdy, ma'am?" We're in the suburbs, not blazing the Great Western Trail.

"Why are y'all letting the boys watch this stuff?" I said.

"It's a classic," they replied in unison, like it was a response they'd rehearsed.

I shook my head and scoffed. "*The Sound of Music*," I said, "now *that* is a classic. Romance, history, great scenery."

"They break into song every two minutes," Kevin complained.

I gave up. Between my husband and his friends, my boys were inundated with lessons in "being a man." I, as the primary influential female in their lives, didn't stand a chance. Being the only female in a household of males means my own interests often take a back seat to theirs. That particular night, I had a sudden and intense need to go out with the girls.

That was years ago, and since then, nothing has changed. In fact, with the addition of Jason, the testosterone-estrogen balance in our house has become even more lopsided. I can't begin to count all the *Power Rangers* shows I've had to watch over the last thirteen years. The producers of that show have devised the best marketing plan ever: update the teens who play the Rangers every year or so, and frequently change the heroes' squadron name, such as Power Rangers DinoThunder or Power Rangers Lightspeed Rescue. *Voila!* Another legion of *Power Rangers* fans. They add a new stripe to the same old action figure, and we go out and buy them again.

I first became aware of the reason moms need to get out of the house often as I watched an episode of *Power Rangers* with my older sons years ago. I became kind of a *Power Rangers* fanatic for a while during the season when they were to reveal who the new Gold Ranger was. Very suspenseful. It was almost like I was watching soap operas in college again.

I recall Kevin coming home to find me standing in front of the TV just as they were about to take off the mask and reveal the Gold Ranger's identity. I was standing there with meat tenderizer in one hand and a raw steak in the other, open-mouthed, as the big moment arrived. Obviously, I'd been in the middle of making dinner when Billy yelled to inform me the moment was upon us, and so I'd dashed into the family room.

My husband took a long look at me, and when I squealed as the new Ranger was revealed, he walked away muttering, "She's one sick puppy." This kind of thing can happen when you're a mother alone in the house with two young boys and no other life to speak of.

Now, with three boys, the situation remains unchanged. I need some "me" time to watch movies like *The Sound of Music* or *You've Got Mail*; to read a novel rather than shoot hoops and pitch baseballs to the guys; to go to a play without having to fit it in around everybody's sports and Scouting schedules; to take a bubble bath at the end of a long day instead of dropping into bed with my sweatshirt and jeans still on.

Sometimes while driving in the car, I enjoy a bit of a respite from the world of testosterone by playing some of my own music. I went through a time when I was hooked on playing a certain song in the car—one from the soundtrack of the Broadway show, *Avenue Q*. I loved the song, "It's a Fine, Fine Line" and listened to it over and over when I first got the CD. It's a song about life and love, and it reaches a soul-tingling crescendo. I realized that even Jason liked listening to this song when one day he said, "Turn it up, Mommy." I heard him singing along with the words, and I realized it was sort of weird for a four-year-old to be singing, "It's a fine, fine line between love and wasting my time." So my music is now restricted to the times I'm in the car by myself.

Finding time for myself in our house is almost impossible. Awhile back, I developed an addiction to the TV show 24. It was the one time a week I could put aside whatever I was doing and relax, totally caught up in the suspense of the plot. I even rented the episodes of previous seasons to know more about the latest developments. I did, however, suffer some side effects; for example, whenever I picked up my cell phone I had an urge to yell into it, "Chloe, can you get me satellite coverage?" or "Damn it—this code is encrypted!"

My 24 routine all started simply enough. It was New Year's Day, the pace of the day was much slower than normal, and football games droned on downstairs in the family room. Jason, who was five then, was coloring in his room, unconcerned with my whereabouts. The two older boys were going back and forth between the football games and playing video games. My husband was asleep on the couch, our dog curled up beside him.

Perhaps I should do some laundry, I thought. But hey, I was only two loads behind instead of my usual five, so it didn't seem that dire of a situation. It suddenly occurred to me that I could sneak away for a few minutes of peace and possibly nobody would notice.

I looked left down the hallway to the family room. I looked right into the kitchen. Nobody was watching. I tiptoed up the stairs and closed the door behind me, retreating into the master bathroom where I had plans to take a long bubble bath. I ran the water and got out the bath oils I'd gotten two Christmases ago but never had time to use. I sank into the foamy bubbles, feeling the tension in my body disappear.

But peace doesn't last long around here.

"Mom!" I heard Jason yell from the hallway. I winced, ignoring him, hoping he'd go downstairs to find his dad. "Mom!" he yelled again.

I sighed. "What!" I shouted back.

He opened the bedroom door and asked, "Where's my Power Rangers SPD coloring book?"

My mind did a quick inventory of the household. "Family room bookcase, second shelf on the left," I said. I was only a little disturbed that I actually knew this information.

Later, while I was getting dressed, I switched on the TV in our bedroom and found some rerun of a show that starred Kiefer Sutherland. Mildly interested, I watched the action as I pulled on my jeans and T-shirt. I learned the show was called 24. Getting more involved in the plot, I crawled into bed and pulled the covers up to my chin.

During the next commercial break, I tried to turn the TV off but found I just couldn't do it. Ten minutes turned into twenty, then thirty. Jack Bauer was in big trouble, and I couldn't take my eyes from the screen. At the end of the thrilling, cliff-hanger show, I discovered the next episode was coming on immediately afterward; my God, I had just stumbled upon a 24 marathon. Did I dare watch another? Pretty soon, my family would realize I was missing and come looking for me. I had to buy some more time.

I raced over and opened the bedroom door, yelling for all to hear, "I'm cleaning out the closet!" This was mother guilt at its finest. I didn't feel right actually relaxing and doing something I wanted to do, so I made up an excuse. After another episode, I began to feel a little strange that nobody had come in after me yet. I opened the door a crack, afraid of what I might find. "Guys?" I shouted.

"They're all outside playing basketball," Kevin replied, groggily.

I stood there for a second, staring at the mound of laundry in front of the washer. I knew what I should do, but I didn't. "Okay," I said, closing the door behind me, relishing my time alone with Jack Bauer.

Finding "me" time is truly a challenge for a woman in a houseful of guys. Admittedly, I've come to appreciate most John Wayne movies, though I'd still rather go see *Camelot* at the theater, all dressed up for once and looking like a woman instead of Mom. And the next time Kevin's friend, Chuck, is over I'll pop *The Sound of Music* into the DVD player, and say to all the guys, "Now, *this* is a classic." Of course, they'll probably all burp simultaneously in response.

5

Ode to the
Family Vacation

— Mom's Vacation Rules for Guys —

1. Three camping trips = one resort vacation for me.

2. When pulling the camper behind us, I am exempt from driving; I can barely handle the SUV by itself.

3. Don't forget to pack your underwear or socks on any more trips; the Boy Scout motto is "Be Prepared," for heaven's sake.

4. Bring along a lot of DVDs to watch in the car. I know it's not good for you, but anything to keep you guys quiet.

5. Please, dear husband, do not ask me to bring along a loaf of bread and some turkey so we can make sandwiches on the road.

6. When we're flying somewhere, remember what happened the last time one of you ate pizza, a hot dog, and a whole pack of M&Ms before the flight.

7. If we're at a Red Sox game and it starts to rain, I get to leave before my hair gets too frizzy.

8. If we're touring another battlefield somewhere and hubby wants to spend two hours in the museum, the boys and I are exempt. We'll be off having some real fun.

9. I get to wear one of those bathing suits with the skirt on it without anyone asking, "Hey what happened to that two-piece you used to have?"

10. If a vacation includes my mother-in-law, we all get a week's supply of valium.

✦ Second Honeymoon

WHEN WE WERE approaching our tenth anniversary, Kevin came to me and said, "Honey, the past ten years have been wonderful, and I want to do something special. Let's go back to California for a second honeymoon."

"Mm-hmmm," I replied skeptically. I knew my cost-conscious husband better than that. Then the reality dawned on me. "You've got business out there, don't you?" I asked.

Kevin looked sheepish. "Yeah, I've been asked to speak at an energy conference. But, hey, it's two free plane tickets and three nights in San Francisco."

Who cares if it was business-related or not? It was still a trip to California. We'd fallen in love with the state on our honeymoon back in 1988 when we drove up the coast from Palm Springs to San Francisco, stopping here and there along the way.

I'll never forget the morning in San Luis Obispo when Kevin went to visit a famous nuclear plant nearby while I showered and got ready to continue our journey. "It's the Diablo Canyon plant!" he'd exclaimed when he first realized we were staying nearby.

I looked at him with a deadpan expression. "Is that supposed to mean something to me?" I asked.

"It's a really famous plant because it sits near a fault line."

"A fault line?" I repeated. "And you want to visit it?" I sure hoped the insurance policy with my new name as the beneficiary had gone through.

"Yeah, you know, I just want to take a few pictures to show the guys back at work."

Someday our grandkids would be going through old photos in our attic and come across pictures of our long-ago honeymoon: the Pacific Ocean, trolley cars in San Francisco, the Diablo Canyon nuclear plant. At least they might realize what their grandmother had had to put up with.

On our honeymoon drive along the coastline, we listened to the radio a lot. One song that was very popular at the time was Tracey Chapman's "Fast Car," and it became one of our favorites as we meandered along the curving highway between the cliffs and the sea. The song itself is actually a bit depressing, about trying to escape a "nowhere" life, but it wasn't the lyrics that captivated us. It was the beautiful, almost haunting music that captivated us as we gazed at the gorgeous California coastline. We loved the song and have always associated it with our honeymoon—that carefree, totally relaxing week in our lives.

The other song that reminds me of our honeymoon is the intro music to the hourly sports update on CNN; Kevin checked Red Sox scores at least three times a night. That, of course, should have been a red flag, but we were already married.

I knew it would be good to go to California again; we'd only been away from Billy and David, then aged seven and four, once before and that was for a family wedding, which I consider to be anything but a vacation. So Kevin and I decided to add a few days to the trip and stay at a bed and breakfast near Monterey.

Kevin flew out a day before me to speak at the energy seminar. When he picked me up at the airport in the rental car, I popped in a cassette tape with "Fast Car" on it. I surprised Kevin with our honeymoon song, a romantic gesture that had become rare for either of us since having kids.

It was strange to behold again the beauty of the same places we'd seen together that first time and odd to think of all we'd come through since then. Standing there on the cliffs overlooking the churning Pacific Ocean, my memories were so vivid that it felt exactly as it had ten years earlier, as though I was gazing at the gorgeous Pacific and jutting cliffs for the first time. It was as if the last ten years had never happened, and time had stood still. Of course, time had not stood still for us but had raced far ahead from our carefree newlywed days. This time there were two young sons waiting back at home for us, staying with relatives.

At every restaurant we visited in California, my eyes automatically gravitated to the children's menu first until I suddenly realized we didn't have the kids with us. It was a funny feeling to be away from them, and I had a moment of guilt that they weren't occupying my every thought the way they usually did. Yet it was also freeing to concentrate on other things for a change. Our getaway granted the time for me to be a different person—perhaps actually a woman—rather than the role of mom I played relentlessly back home.

Fisherman's Wharf in San Francisco was just as we remembered it, full of life and fun. We drove across the Golden Gate Bridge to a park that provided a stunning view of the city skyline, and the famous bridge glistened in the setting sun. We made our first visit to The Cliff House, a restaurant with a huge window looking out over the ocean. The view was breathtaking.

After leaving San Francisco, we drove south on the Pacific Coast Highway to Monterey to stay at the Martine Inn, a bed and breakfast by the sea. It was incredibly peaceful, and I felt as if I'd been submerged into another world. No sibling rivalry fights, no "Mom, you know what?" stories, and no constant ringing of the telephone.

We called the boys on Sunday, which was Mother's Day, to see how they were doing. I expected to hear how much they missed us, especially since it was only the second time we had ever left them. But all they could talk about was the "awesome" toys their aunts and grandmothers had bought them. Finally, after Billy's three-minute description of the plot of his new *Godzilla Versus Mothra* videotape, I asked, "Do you know what day this is?"

A short silence. "Mother's Day," he replied.

Another silence. "So...?" I asked.

"Oh, yeah. Happy Mother's Day," he said. Ah yes, a Mother's Day greeting as heartfelt as they come. So nice to be appreciated. I felt a little disappointed, but mostly, I was relieved they were getting along fine without me.

That afternoon we took another drive along the curving highway, heading farther south toward Big Sur. The road hugged the coastline, and the drive itself was spectacular. We stopped at the Rocky Point Restaurant just south of Carmel and had lunch on the ocean terrace with a view of the famous Bixby Bridge that crosses between the cliffs. Absolutely stunning.

Romantic beyond words. I thought again of our honeymoon when our love was new, when we had first shared this same awe-inspiring vista.

Kevin was quiet, peering down over the cliff to the sea below, lost deep in thought. I wondered if he was reminiscing, too. I touched him gently on his arm. "What are you thinking about?" I asked softly.

"One little earthquake and we're toast," he said.

So much for romance.

Later, as we sat on the terrace along with the families celebrating Mother's Day, I eavesdropped on a conversation between an elderly woman and her daughter-in-law. "Those were the best days," the elderly woman said. "Raising our kids . . . those were the best days."

A chill ran up my spine because I suddenly knew the woman was right. Those are the best days. And they were going by much too quickly. It had been a terrific vacation, but I couldn't wait to return home to my boys.

✦ A-Camping We Will Go

My husband's dream has always been to buy a camper. My dream has been to go to one of those writer's conferences at the beach where they give you massages and gourmet food, a hundred miles away from kids' homework and sibling arguments. So several years ago we finally did it: We bought a camper.

Have you ever noticed how a mom's dreams take a back seat to everybody else's? Alas, the conference at the beach will have to wait, at least until camping days are over.

Camping is one of those things that a lot of guys, including mine, like to do, and unfortunately we moms have to go along with it, or we'll spoil their fun. "Come on, Mom, it'll be a great family activity," my sons tell me, making me feel guilty if I say no.

So a-camping we will go. Actually, it's not "real" camping like sleeping in a tent. My husband adores that kind of camping ("Just a pack on your back with your sleeping bag and nature around for miles, ahhh," Kevin will say, his eyes closed as if in meditation), but he knew he could only push me so far. Our camper is a little mini-home complete with stove, microwave, bathroom, beds, air conditioning, and heat. And TV. Ahhh, yes, nature. Now we're ready to camp out in the wild—or at least poolside on the shores of Myrtle Beach.

The one drawback is the size of the bathroom—can you say "microscopic?" When Kevin first showed me the tiny room with a sink, shower, and toilet crammed into the space the trash can occupied in our bathroom at home, I was skeptical.

I glanced around the room quickly, looking for something good to say, not wanting to burst Kevin's bubble. I couldn't even comment on the wallpaper because there wasn't enough wall to put paper on.

"Well," I finally said, "it'll make me appreciate old age."

He frowned. "Why?"

"One day when I have osteoporosis I'll finally be able to stand up in the shower." He didn't crack a smile, perhaps because he realized I was right. Or more likely, he was perturbed. I knew I'd better watch myself, or he could trade in the camper for one of those blasted tents that require an advanced degree in physics to put up.

At least the camper *has* a bathroom. The thought of having to trudge through the woods at 2 a.m. to use a smelly, unheated outhouse with bugs on the floor and no toilet paper does not thrill me.

Since people name their boats, I toyed with the idea of giving our camper a name. But I wasn't sure what we should call it. Hmmm…somehow *Husband's Mid-Life Crisis* had a good ring to it. I knew Kevin was itching to go camping and reclaim some of his fondly remembered Scouting days while instilling a love of camping in our three sons.

I first noticed this camping desire of his during a December ice storm a few months before we bought the camper. The storm knocked out power across the region. I should have known Kevin would look at it as an adventure. His eyes sparkled when he realized we'd have to all sleep overnight without lights or heat. The Eagle Scout in him roared to life as he envisioned camping in the family room, relying only on his survival skills to keep us safe.

I, on the other hand, dropped out after my first year of Brownies, unable to handle the sewing, the crafts, and, yes— the camping. As he came in from the garage, carrying a lantern and lumpy sleeping bags, I watched in misery, thinking of the news reports of people flocking to hotels that had generators. I thought of them in their toasty, well-lit rooms, watching TV and reading into the night, dialing up room service for a sandwich, sending the kids to swim in the indoor pool. But, regretfully, that was not in our future with a past-his-prime Eagle Scout for a leader.

We stockpiled all the flashlights in the house, although some of them had no batteries, like most of the stuff in our house. Jason, who was two and a half, was upset all day, due to video withdrawal, I'd thought. In the late afternoon, however, I realized he had a fever. I brought out the red Tylenol and squirted a teaspoonful down Jason's throat, only to have him spit most of it right back on me.

Billy and David were tired after a day of storm debris yard work, any thrill of adventure rapidly disappearing. And Kevin, in turn, was disappointed by their eroding enthusiasm. We ate some of the food in the refrigerator before it went bad and put the rest of it in a cooler outside. Afterward, we hunkered down in our sleeping bags for a long night. Since Jason wanted me to sleep beside him on the floor, Eagle Scout lucked out and took the couch. As the cold night wore on, it became obvious that he'd been absent at the Scouts meeting where they learned how to rub two sticks together to make a fire.

I had a rough night lying beside my restless toddler. As the sun finally rose, I shouted, "Thank goodness, it's morning!" All I heard in reply was snoring from the couch.

Later, when we realized we'd have to spend another night without power, I turned to Kevin, stating emphatically, "I don't know what you're going to do, but the boys and I are out of here. Hotel here we come."

He looked sheepish. "The radio says they're all booked," he informed me. Mercifully, the power came back on that afternoon, saving us from another cold, dark night, and probably also saving our marriage.

So the December adventure was a prelude, a warning of what was to come. We had been receiving *Trailer Life* magazine in the mail for about six months, so I did have an inkling of what Kevin had on his mind. Then there were those RVers

Are Us websites I'd noticed he'd been on, which also piqued my curiosity.

As we drove to pick up our spiffy new "home away from home," even I started to get excited about camping. I have to admit—ever since I was a kid and saw that episode of *The Brady Bunch* where everybody piled in the station wagon and went camping in the Grand Canyon, there was a certain allure to camping out under the stars. I remember thinking to myself back then, "What a cool family vacation!" Little did I know Kevin's plan was more like crossing the country for free by parking the camper in Wal-Mart parking lots at night. (Yes, unfortunately, I'm serious.)

Looking toward the future when Jason would be older, I could vaguely see a time when my husband would take all three of the boys camping without me. A guys' weekend away, a light at the end of the proverbial tunnel. If I could only hang on and pretend I liked camping for a few years, the camper would someday become *my* ticket to freedom, as well. I was salivating at the mere idea.

While the salesperson was guiding us through our buyer's tour of the camper, I was struck by the reality of it. Setting up a camper required more work than I ever imagined. There were towing and hitching lessons, more details than you'd ever want to know about sewer systems, and lots of other tidbits of information. This was more than a walk-through; we were there all afternoon learning about electrical hookups, double sway-cross bars, and winterizing with chemicals. Kevin was actually taking notes and videotaping the salesman's instructions. I could envision Kevin entertaining our next dinner guests with this informational home video. Hell, they'd be begging to watch Jason's baptism tape again and again rather than having to sit through *Trailer Life for Dummies* that Kevin found so fascinating.

By the third hour, my eyes were glazed over. It was almost like being back in Algebra class. I was hoping my husband understood all of these instructions because I'd given up long before.

As I sat there zombied out, I came to a painful realization. The truth of the phrase "home away from home" finally hit me, and I sat straight up from my slumped position and swallowed hard. No! Having that nice stove in the camper meant I'd have to cook on vacations, and having no hotel maid service meant I'd have to do laundry. Do you know how many towels our family goes through in two days? I started panicking and second-guessing our decision, dreaming of stacks of white hotel towels folded neatly in the bathroom, placed there by someone other than me. Why, this would be just like home only in a smaller space. Vacation *was* the operative word here after all, wasn't it?

But the papers were signed. More importantly, Eagle Scout was smiling, beaming from ear to ear. I took a deep breath and mustered up my courage. "Hey," I thought to myself, "if the Brady Bunch can do it, so can I." My spirits came crashing down, however, when I remembered the Bradys had taken their maid, Alice, along on the trip, too. Mrs. Brady was no fool. Then I wondered if there were at least some kind of merit badge I could get for this.

✦ Baseball and Battlefields

The sun was blazing hot, and sweat streamed down my face. "One more pitch, Mom," David begged. He was ten and had somehow talked me into helping with batting practice.

"Okay," I said, "just one, and then we've got to go." I got into my pitcher's pose—er, I mean stance—and tossed the ball to David. Smack! The ball sailed high into the air and across the field. I started to race for it, then stopped. "Jason, run and go get it," I told my youngest, who was four at the time. He took off, eager to fetch, undaunted by the fact the ball was a quarter of a mile away. Kids that age are handy to have around sometimes.

My husband had taken Billy to a Scouting event, and so I had to—I mean, I had the privilege of taking our two youngest boys to a local Little League field to practice.

Jason brought the ball back and then immediately picked up his bat. "My turn now." He'd already had numerous "turns," but being the swell mom that I am, I continued to pitch. Even though Jason was not as good of a sport as David and accused me of "throwing crooked," we still had fun anyway. And I had completed my duty of being a cool mom, although I realized my pitching arm wasn't what it used to be. Or my knees.

All I'm going to say is that my boys had better come visit me in the rest home.

When the batting practice was over, we got back home to find Kevin had returned from the Scouting meeting and was in the recliner watching yet another documentary on D-day. I'm a history buff, too, and can appreciate the sacrifice and drama of what happened that day on the beaches of Normandy, but how many times can one person watch historians draw maps of the invasion on a chalkboard?

I sighed and went out to the garage to put away the baseball bats. This is what I'd come to expect from life with my husband and sons: baseball and battlefields. Kevin has always had a fascination with war, like most men do. He never was in the service, but I sincerely believe he spends half his waking hours wondering what combat would have been like and what kind of soldier he would have been. I half expect to come home one day and find him dressed in a uniform with stars on the shoulder, demanding I call him Patton or Ike. I draw the line at saluting him, though. Not unless he comes through with that new leather furniture for our family room or a surprise getaway to Palm Springs.

Or maybe I'll wake in a panic one morning to find our alarm clock gone, replaced by bugles and a resounding version of reveille. His addiction to being a Boy Scout leader was starting to make sense.

When a commercial came on the History Channel, he stood and stretched and started into the kitchen. As he passed by me he said with a finger pointing in the air for emphasis, "One day I *will* go to Normandy. If it's the last thing I do before I die." See? The drama of life and death was really getting to him. Did I detect the glimmer of a tear in his eye?

"Okay," I replied. "I'd like to go there, too." I patted his arm, hoping to calm him, reassure him that someday we'd make the journey.

"Would you really go?" he asked.

I was hurt. Genuinely hurt. I had never given him a reason to think I didn't want to go to Normandy when he'd brought it up before. Besides, I was the same woman who spent our fall vacation in Virginia visiting the site of Lee's surrender at Appomattox and the National D-Day museum in Bedford. The same woman who spent our spring vacation in our camper in Gettysburg where we took a four-hour driving tour of cemeteries and monuments galore; where we took photos of the boys sitting on cannons; where we gazed solemnly at the site of Pickett's Charge.

I was the same woman who, in Boston, waited in line with rowdy, bored four-year-old Jason—even though I had to pee really bad—just to get on Old Ironsides, a ship used primarily in the Revolutionary War. I was the same woman who toured Fort McHenry, Fort Macon, and every Civil War museum in Virginia. How dare he question my loyalty? Of course, I would go with him to Normandy. It would be educational and inspiring, the trip of a lifetime. Besides, since we'd be flying overseas, there would be no chance he could insist we stay in our camper. *Gasp!* We'd just have to stay in a nice hotel for once.

Yep, baseball and battlefields. The undeviating themes of O'Donnell family leisure. It's the lot I've drawn in life, and I accept it. Every year we take a vacation that combines both elements; we travel to a Red Sox baseball game in Boston or in Baltimore and take in the historic sites along the way. I do like this idea in theory, but year after year, it starts getting a little old. Just once, why don't we take off to Broadway or Rome or Chicago instead? But, no, the tradition has begun, and so it stands. And as the female minority in my household, I'm always outvoted by the guys anyway. So baseball and battlefields it will be.

I have to prepare myself for the day my sons will be afflicted by the same war obsession as my husband. Already, on Memorial Day of every year, Kevin makes the guys sit down and watch *Midway* until their eyes pop out. They seem interested in all the history, but they're not quite to the point of watching war movie marathons. There was one Memorial Day when Billy and David were about ten and seven, when they came running to me in a panic, yelling, "Mom, don't let him make us watch *Midway* again!" They were hiding behind me, crouching, fear on their faces. Part of a mother's job is to intervene in situations like this, so I stepped in to save the poor fellows. I patted Kevin on the back and told him, "It's a fine movie, honey, but we all think you've gone a little over the edge."

"Really?" he asked, the expressions on the boys' faces now bringing him back to reality.

I decided he could handle the truth. "Yep. Like a California mudslide barreling down the cliffs, completely out of control. AWOL. You're gone, dear."

The next day Kevin went to Blockbuster and came back with a DVD and a bag of microwave popcorn. "What movie did you get?" I asked, fooled into believing we'd have some time to relax and unwind together. Then I saw the title: *The Sands of Iwo Jima*. A John Wayne World War II movie. It appeared that we'd be planning our next vacation for Japan.

I wracked my mind for an excuse not to watch. "Sorry, Kev," I said, grabbing a glove off the table. "I have to go pitch baseballs to the guys."

✦ Snapshots of Disney

Before our family's trip to Disney World in the fall of 2003, Jason, who was three at the time, made it clear he wanted to go soon and that he was having a difficult time waiting for our big trip. A few months before we left, Jason was looking through a photo album of pictures from an earlier Disney trip we had taken with our two older boys. He came across a photo of his brothers with Buzz Lightyear and Woody, the cowboy from *Toy Story*. He mumbled sadly, "I want to be in that picture." Then he stood up on the couch—I'm not making this up—and tried to jump into the photo. He immediately realized it wasn't going to work and started to cry, saying, "I'm too big."

Soon after that incident, I was picking up Billy and David from a Scout meeting at our church. It was nighttime, and bright lights lit up the towering white steeple of a neighboring church. In the back seat, Jason exclaimed, "Mommy, there it is!"

I glanced out the window and asked, "There what is?"

"Disney World!" he shouted gleefully. That's when I noticed the steeple did look somewhat like Cinderella's Castle, the most famous landmark at Disney, which he'd seen in books and at the beginnings of movies. I smiled at Jason's excitement, assuring him that he would get to see the castle in person soon.

When we finally arrived in Orlando a few months later, it turned out to be everything Jason had imagined. His favorite was the Buzz Lightyear ride, and he posed with all the characters, not showing a bit of fear.

Disney was fun for Billy and David, too, but since they had been there a number of times, some of the magic had worn off.

As I watched Billy, twelve, and David, nine, with their little brother at the park, I couldn't help reflecting back on our earlier trips to Disney.

In his younger days, Billy's favorite character was Mickey Mouse. His T-shirts, toys, and videotapes all featured Mickey (I would have savored this Mickey phase a bit more if I had known then that his Power Rangers phase was just around the corner). Naturally, when we first got to Disney, three-year-old Billy wanted to see Mickey right away, but when we entered the park, we couldn't locate the giant mouse. When he finally saw Mickey standing on Main Street in the Magic Kingdom, Billy's eyes lit up like I'd never seen before. He grinned and walked slowly up to Mickey, not quite believing the moment had arrived. Billy hugged Mickey, and they posed for a picture that now sits in a frame at home.

David was just a baby then, and he slept in my arms through all the shows, which was remarkable. At that time, Kevin and I were still in control of our family, and there wasn't nearly the amount of stress that we have now.

Later that week, we visited Mickey in his dressing room, where both boys posed for a photo. We weren't sure how nine-month-old David would react, being so young. I was prepared to grab him off Mickey's lap as soon as the first tear appeared. But tears didn't fall. Instead, David turned and stared up at Mickey, a curious and innocent look on his chubby face, probably wondering exactly what this furry, bow-tied thing was. Then he reached up and touched Mickey's cheek, caressing it lovingly. I snapped the camera.

On our next trip to Disney, David was three and Billy six. As we drove to Florida, we passed a pulp and paper mill with an awful stench emanating from it. My husband decided to have some fun teasing David, so he wrinkled up his nose and said, "Oh man, David, cut it out. Phewee!"

David stuck his lips out, pouting, and said, "I didn't do it." This was just the beginning of the "passing-gas era" that still continues in our home. Now, though, David is more likely to take credit for it instead of denying the blame.

That time at Disney, Billy was really into collecting autographs from all the characters, and it took our entire (blanking) trip to locate the elusive Scrooge McDuck. Billy's deep interest in the characters surprised me; on a trip to Carowinds Amusement Park a year earlier, he'd told me he knew Scooby Doo was just somebody dressed up because he'd seen the zipper on the costume. I felt like reminding him of that during our exhaustive search for Scrooge McDuck, but I just didn't have the heart. He still liked Mickey, but it wasn't the same all-encompassing adoration he'd had when he was three.

We took our third excursion to the Magic Kingdom when I was pregnant with Jason. It was the only time we flew down instead of driving, and despite being as big as Shamu the whale, I really enjoyed it. David had also recently broken his arm, and he had to wear a cast he wasn't supposed to get wet. Between his arm and my belly, it was a challenge to go on the rides, but we made the best of it. (I got to sit in the shade and drink lemonade while Kevin stood in all the long lines. I guess the pregnancy thing did have its fringe benefits).

So on Jason's first trip to Disney, all these memories of my older boys were running through my head. I wanted to make the magic come alive for Jason, so that when we looked back on photos of his first time at Disney, we'd see the happiness in his eyes.

This trip was a little different because it was the first one in our camper. Yes, we drove from Raleigh, North Carolina, to Central Florida towing our travel trailer. This meant we couldn't stop at any gas station along the way unless it had ample parking and plenty of space to turn around.

Unfortunately, this limited the use of restrooms, too. There was one particular stretch of highway that didn't have an acceptable turn-around spot for miles. Jason had just been potty-trained, but the bathroom situation was still, shall we say, precarious. If he said he had to go, he definitely had to go. There was no "warning time" built in here.

Kevin and I got into one of our worst arguments ever when Jason told us, "I have to poop now," and Kevin said there was no place to turn the camper around so we had to keep going.

"He has to poop, Kev!" I screamed. "This is non-negotiable."

"There's nowhere to turn around!" Kevin shouted back.

"Pull over somewhere, 'cause he's got to go!"

"Where?" he yelled, as we passed yet another exit with a gas station.

"Back there?" I suggested, as I watched the gas station disappear in the rearview mirror. But Kevin claimed he wouldn't have had enough space at that station to get the camper safely in and out.

"When you bought this thing I had no idea it was going to be harder to maneuver than a yacht," I remarked. I looked at Jason's face and took a deep breath. "I'm going to have to bring out the potty chair."

"Oh, no, not the potty chair," Billy and David moaned from the back.

"It's our last resort," I said, "or we're going to have a mess in here."

"How are you going to put him on the potty chair if the car is still moving, Mom?" Billy asked incredulously.

I looked him in the eyes. "It won't be easy," I said.

Luckily, just at that time, Kevin spotted a truck stop with a huge parking lot and a driveway that circled behind the building, providing an easy place to turn around. "Wait," he said, "I see a place to stop up here."

"Eureka!" I shouted, feeling every bit as thrilled as Lewis and Clark must have when they first saw the Pacific.

My travel tip for you (if you don't already know from experience): Don't travel long distances with a recently potty-trained child and a husband who's just learning to pull a camper. It's a bad, bad mix.

But all in all, Disney worked its magic once more, and we went home with Jason's own pictures to add to the photo album.

✦ Pool Moms

Our family has traveled to the beach on vacation quite a bit. Usually, this involves relaxing by a pool or on the sand (as much as you can relax with three boys) and eating lots of seafood. There was one rare beach trip where we actually stayed in a hotel instead of the infamous camper. Unfortunately, the brochure had depicted the rundown hotel as a posh resort; we were very disappointed when we got there and found ourselves victims of false advertising. Kevin had to rub it in by saying, "With our camper, at least you always know what you're going to get."

The pool was pretty nice, so we spent most of our time there. But I'm not ordinarily a "pool" person, on vacation or at home. I enjoy the occasional dip in the pool, but for some people—the "pool people," as I call them—it is a way of life. They've got it down to a precision exercise, while I struggle with the details of bad tan lines and constantly adjusting patio furniture. You know the people I'm talking about: the bronze teenage lifeguards who look like they could swim before they walked, who peer through their sunglasses, keeping a watchful eye on the water from their chair; the kids who frequent the pool every day during the summer months, swimming laps, playing Marco Polo, and bonding with other "pool kids;" and of course, the "pool mom," who takes her young kids to the pool, calmly rubs sunscreen on them without any one fidgeting or getting it in their eyes, then pulls out a best-selling novel to read while the kids frolic, with the organized cooler of healthy snacks waiting beside her. She has on a coordinating swimsuit and cover-up, complete with matching tote bag. Her hair never frizzes even after she hops in for a swim, and it dries in the sun.

I am in awe of the "pool people," especially those who frequent the neighborhood swimming pools regularly. I enjoy taking the boys to our local swimming pool, but after a few hours, I'm ready to go home for a shower, dry clothes, and air conditioning. It's not an everyday event, mainly due to our busy schedules—and also the fact that I am not a "pool person."

Billy and David were in year-round school during elementary and middle school, so our summer was only four short weeks, leaving us to fit in sports camps and vacation, too. So we have not been regulars at the pool, except during the weeks of swim lessons, which give me an incentive to go.

Over the years, I've been the one who usually takes the boys to their swimming lessons. Every mother knows how it feels to be at those early swimming lessons, watching your child struggle, and knowing it would take only one little slip and they'd go under. When my boys took swimming lessons, I'd always be right there, ready to slip off my shoes and jump in to rescue them if something went wrong (forgetting all about the fact that I myself almost drowned in a wave pool at a water park).

When I take Jason to his lessons now, I make a point of giving him the "thumbs up." This bit of encouragement stems from an awful experience we had when he was three. He cried the entire swimming lesson, clinging to his instructor and yelling that the water was too cold. And it was. I put my toe in the water, and it literally took my breath away. It was an overcast morning in early June, and it was a bit chilly. Eventually, I was banished to the pool house because the instructor thought it might help Jason calm down. But it made it worse. He was asked to go to a lower-level class, but the water was still so ice cold that it made his teeth chatter. (We decided to sign up for lessons at an indoor pool instead, which went fine.)

So, after that experience at the chilly pool, Jason always looks for me when he's swimming, and I know it's important to him that I pay attention. I don't bring books to read or work to do because I want to be there for him.

Kevin will take him to the lessons if I'm teaching a writing class. When Jason was five, Kevin brought him home from the pool one day, and I asked how he had done.

"Okay, I guess," Kevin replied.

Then Jason told the true story. "Mom," he said, "Dad fell asleep at my swim lessons. He didn't even watch me." Jason looked up at me with sad eyes and a sullen face.

"You fell asleep?" I asked Kevin. "You're supposed to watch him." Men just don't understand the importance of such things.

All of our sons have had swimming lessons, but still our family doesn't spend a lot of time at the pool. To the non-pool person like me, the whole experience can be more of a hassle than anything else

But it's never a hassle for the pool mom. That cooler of snacks she brings for her kids always contains some kind of fresh fruit like grapes, bananas, or even kiwis, and maybe some cheese cubes and juice. The pool mom is very organized and makes time to pack nutritious snacks instead of forgetting like me and having to scrounge for coins in the bottom of my pocketbook, so my kids can buy a hot dog.

Then there's the attire. The "pool mom" has the perfect swimsuit and seems very comfortable in it. Excuse me, but I find it difficult to relax poolside if every time I get up, the bottom part of my bathing suit rises up to where, as Andy Griffith might say, "it ought not should be risin'." Why can guys wear swim trunks that come down to their knees, while women always have to worry about how much of what is showing? Come on, ladies, you know you do. One-piece suits, bikinis, tankinis—whatever they call them—the bottom line is they're basically underwear, folks. We wouldn't go to the mall like that, but just because somebody once said it's okay to wear them around water, we all go along with it.

Add to this the fact that my family has problems swimming in chlorinated water because it bothers our eyes immensely, making them red and sore the rest of the day. Exactly what is chlorine anyway, and is it totally safe? Pool people never wonder about that or have red eyes; it's like chlorine acts as a natural skin cleanser or something for them.

Since we don't spend much time poolside on vacations, it's sometimes challenging to keep the guys busy. Kevin seems to think if we take the camper, there are lots of things to do at the beach campgrounds. Let's see…I can think of cooking, cleaning, laundry. For a while, whenever we went to the beach, Kevin would volunteer to take all the dirty clothes to the laundromat close to where we stayed. I should have been suspicious of his eagerness to do this, but I wasn't; I was just glad the laundry was getting done.

Then one morning when the boys were driving me crazy with their bickering, I decided to walk down to the laundromat, where Kevin had been for over an hour. Lo and behold, there he was, sitting there, drinking a Dr. Pepper, watching sports on a TV, and flipping through a magazine. Ah, so this is why he had so willingly volunteered. He knew he'd been caught.

I put some coins in for another dry cycle, picked up *People* magazine, and sent Kevin back to the pool for lifeguard duty with the boys. This time, I hoped he would stay awake.

6

Wisdom, Thou Cometh at a High Price

— Lessons I've Learned While Raising Boys —

1. Don't let your boys get away with giving lame answers and opinions such as, "I liked it" or "It was good." Dig deeper; it's in there.

2. Every now and then, letting them "sleep in" is exactly what they need.

3. It's imperative that you hang a huge calendar right by the phone and fill it up with all the meetings, practices, birthday parties, field trips, and games. Their schedule will become your schedule. Don't allow the schedules to get too busy.

4. Sometimes you have to take a deep breath and advocate for your son.

5. Sometimes you have to hold your tongue and let him advocate for himself.

6. Boys don't use umbrellas.

7. They do grow up fast, but never hesitate to hug them (when no one else is looking, of course).

8. Talk to your sons about their interests or how their day went or what they're feeling about world events. I find the best time to "connect" with my boys is when they are settling down for the night.

9. The best gift you can give your son is helping him build a foundation of faith and family.

10. Have fun with your son, whether it's playing football together in the yard, going to a movie, playing with blocks, or cheering for his favorite team. Treasure those moments.

♦ Playing by the Rules

Sometimes life's best lessons don't come easy. I've always tried to teach my sons the importance of playing by the rules, but along the way they also have to learn for themselves that doing the right thing doesn't always mean everything will turn out fair. It's a lesson that's tough for parents to see their children learn. There have been a few times in particular that my two oldest sons have had to learn this lesson the hard way.

The first time took place when Billy was a seven-year-old Cub Scout and was racing his car in the Pinewood Derby, the biggest Scouting event of the year. The boys build cars from small blocks of pine; they whittle and shape their cars and then paint them. Usually, the dads help out with this, showing the young Scouts how to do it safely and leaving wood shavings all over the kitchen floor.

The boys race these cars down a steeply sloped track, and all finishes are precisely timed by a computer. During the month before the race, Billy and my husband tried out the car at the official derby trials. Billy's car ran very fast, and no adjustments were needed. The Friday night before the race, there was another opportunity to test the cars on the track. Again, Billy's car did extremely well.

The morning of the race, Billy was very excited. The gymnasium was packed with a roped-off seating section for spectators. Billy's car won its first race. Smooth sailing. In the second race, Billy's car jumped the track for some reason, and they had to run it again. He went on to win with another fast time. Billy's car was in second place out of about fifty Scouts, and we were all very hopeful he would win, especially Billy. Then in the third race, Billy's car jumped the track again. Strange. It hadn't done that in all the many trial runs it had taken, and no changes had been made. They re-ran the race. Again, Billy's car swerved off the track.

All action stopped as the officials consulted the rule book. Then the Scout leader picked up a microphone and announced that when a car jumps the track twice within a race, the car must be disqualified from the whole event. I felt sick, and I knew Kevin did too. The best word I can think of to describe Billy's face at that moment is *bewildered*; his blue eyes wide under the bill of his Scout cap. It was so unexpected, such a fluke, after his car had done so well in trials.

He came and stood next to me, and I put my arm around his waist. I wanted to hug him tight, but I knew he wouldn't want me to do that in front of his friends. His dad came over and said, "Billy, it's okay. It wasn't your fault. It was just one of those things."

Billy's lips quivered. Kevin patted him on the shoulder and then had to go back to his Scout leader duties. I asked Billy if he wanted to go outside. He shook his head, never taking his eyes off the continuing car races in front of him. It was like he was hypnotized.

"They have pizza," I told him. "Want some?" He shook his

head again. So we just stood there awhile in silence, my arm around him. The hurt look on his face is hard to shake from my memory. This wasn't the trivial kind of disappointment that happened when I wouldn't take them to a store when they wanted to go. This was the deep-down, gut-wrenching kind of disappointment.

But we were more proud of our son that day than if he had won first place. Billy never cried or complained, just took it stoically.

That was the first time Kevin and I had seen one of our sons get hurt by wanting something so badly but not getting a chance at it because of circumstances.

There was another learning episode that also involved the Pinewood Derby race. David was in the fourth grade, and his car had won second place in his Cub Scout Pack race, thus earning him a spot to race at the district derby at the mall on a Saturday. He'd won the entire district race the year before, but there were a couple of other cars this particular year that were running a little faster than David's. As the race neared its end, David was in third place and hoping to hold onto it because they only gave trophies for the top three spots.

In the next race, David's car didn't do well at all, quite the opposite of what it had been doing. Visions of Billy's earlier Pinewood experience replayed in our heads as we wondered why David's car had slowed down so dramatically.

Then another bad race, and David's car was out of contention for a trophy. While the final races went on, Kevin got a chance to examine David's car and saw a chip in the front of the car, definitely enough of a problem to slow it down. "What happened to it?" I asked Kevin.

Kevin shrugged. "David says he dropped it before the race." We were glad David had at least won the previous year, but of course, disappointed that his car had been damaged.

After the race, I asked David why he hadn't told us earlier that he'd dropped his car. Perhaps we could have fixed it.

My introverted David mumbled, "I didn't know it was damaged."

"How hard did you drop it?"

"I didn't exactly drop it. A kid knocked it out of my hands."

"What?" I asked, alarmed.

"I dropped it because a kid hit it."

"On purpose?"

"Yeah. He laughed about it."

My blood started to boil. "David, why didn't you tell someone?"

"I don't know," he answered meekly.

"What kid was it?" I asked, my eyes darting around the room. David pointed him out, and I went ballistic. It was the kid who had ended up winning third place.

When I told Kevin about this, he went nuts, too. But we had to try to contain our anger—after all, this was just a Pinewood Derby, not the Daytona 500. We didn't want to stir up trouble or come off sounding like sore losers, yet we didn't want David to be taken advantage of, either.

Kevin ended up writing a short note to the Scouting district just to encourage them to reiterate the rules of sportsmanship to the guys in future races. We told David to put the incident behind him, but to learn from it that he should speak up for his rights. If David had not won the top award the previous year, perhaps we would have taken this further.

Another time we experienced a lesson about life was in 2001, when we were on vacation in Boston. As my family and I stood in the press box high above the field, the skyline of the city provided a beautiful backdrop for Fenway Park, home of pro baseball's Boston Red Sox. We had tickets that night to watch the Sox take on the Toronto Blue Jays, and Billy, ten, and David, seven, wanted to take the guided tour of historic Fenway that's offered to fans. It was a chance to see the field from up in the executive offices and the press box; to touch the famed Green Monster, the high left field wall; and most importantly, to sit in the Red Sox dugout where some of baseball's best have awaited their turn to bat since it was built in 1912.

Kevin, a lifelong Boston fan, used to go with his parents on vacations to New England and would visit Fenway Park when he was a boy. Naturally, my sons have become huge Red Sox fans like their dad.

As we stood in the press box overlooking the stadium, Billy stared down at the field. He was mesmerized by Boston's ace pitcher Pedro Martinez, who was doing some practice pitching. Martinez was one of the best pitchers in all of baseball. Billy couldn't wait for the field part of the tour so he could be near him.

Then Martinez left the field. Billy sighed, disappointed. He quickly brightened, though, and grabbed my sleeve, exclaiming, "Mom, they left one of the baseballs Pedro pitched on the field! Do you think I could have it?"

I looked down and saw a lone baseball lying on the grass near the edge of the field. I didn't want to disappoint him, but I told him I was sure there were rules about it and that anybody else who spotted that ball probably wanted it, too. As we walked down to the field, the tour guide informed us of the strict rules about staying off the grass since they were preparing it for the game. "If you step on the grass," she told us, "you will be escorted out."

When we got to the side of the field, the ball was still there, tempting my son to run out and grab it. "You have to ask first, Billy," I reminded him. He went over to the tour guide and politely asked if he could have the ball and was told an emphatic *no* because not even tour guides were allowed on the grass. The ball had to stay there. The disappointment showed on his face immediately. As we listened to the tour guide talk about the Green Monster, Billy still eyed that ball. He ached for it.

The tour ended soon afterward. As we left the field, Billy and I were following behind the rest of the crowd. Suddenly, a teenage boy scooted six or seven steps onto the field, grabbed the Pedro ball, dropped it in his backpack, and walked out. Billy turned and looked at me like I'd led him astray—I, who had insisted he play by the rules. I felt terrible. I made it a point to mention what happened to the tour guide, although I didn't point out the culprit, who was long gone anyway. I just wanted her to acknowledge to Billy that he had done the right thing. Instead, she offered a quick, "Oh, that's too bad," not quite the support I was hoping for.

These lessons of life are usually tougher on the parents than on the kids because, as parents, we have to watch our children suffer consequences not of their own making. In the long run, I'd like to think these experiences will pay off for our boys as they navigate life's rough waters, and that's more valuable than any racing trophy or baseball could ever be.

✦ Saying "I'm Sorry"

Erich Segal, the author of the 1970s non-fiction bestseller, *Love Story*, did the human race a disservice when he coined the phrase, "Love means never having to say you're sorry." A nice, catchy ending for a tearjerker, but in reality, relationships depend on the use of these words. In real relationships, we need to hear "I'm sorry" from time to time.

When Billy was in kindergarten and learning to spell, I recall an argument he had with me, though its details now escape me. Kevin and I sent him to his room, where later I found him curled up in his bed, fast asleep. But on his drawing easel beside his bed were written the words, "Im srwe Mom. I love you." In that moment, the argument itself became unimportant. He had felt badly about what happened and wanted me to know he was sorry. I tore that page form his drawing pad and saved it and still keep it in a chest in our bedroom.

When David was four, he apologized to me for hitting his older brother. Then I commanded him to "tell Billy you're sorry, too."

David grinned and said to Billy, "You're sorry, too." Another blow in the battle of wits they continually fight. Years ago, whenever David got in trouble, Billy would start singing the theme song to the show, *Cops*: "Bad boy, bad boy, whatcha gonna do when they come for you?" This always made David furious.

David used to be told to say he was sorry for so many things he did that he naturally associated saying "I'm sorry" with guilt. He didn't understand there are other times we say we're sorry to empathize with people. This became abundantly clear to me when a family friend was killed in a car accident back when David was almost four. I explained to David that I was going to the funeral home because a friend had been killed, and I was going to tell his family I was sorry.

He lowered his head, then looked at me with wide eyes. "Did you do it?" he asked. He actually thought that since I was going to say I was sorry, I must have killed the person. I assured him that I had not killed anyone and made a vow to show David saying "I'm sorry" can be used simply to express sympathy to someone, not to apologize for doing a wrong against somebody.

I recall another incident in a gift shop at Fort McHenry, the birthplace of the national anthem. Seven-year-old Billy and I were browsing in the shop when a woman with a loud, nasal voice tapped him on the shoulder and asked, "Did you tell your Mommy you broke a bell?" Billy looked at her, confused. Then I looked at her, confused.

I asked Billy, "Did you break something in here?"

"No, Mom," he said, his eyes teary.

But the woman persisted again in her loud voice. "Oh yes, he did," she said. "And I just thought he should be honest and tell you about it." She walked over to some trinkets and said, "Here are the bells right over here." By this point, other people had heard her accusations and were watching us. I believed my son because he'd never before given me cause to doubt him. "This is where he broke a bell."

Then the store clerk, who had been busy with a customer, looked up from the cash register and said, "Oh no, that wasn't the boy who broke the bell—it was some other kid in a gray T-shirt."

Relief washed over me. The woman with the nasal voice turned to me, gave me a quick smile, and mumbled, "Oh, I'm sorry." She turned away and continued shopping. After the embarrassment she caused Billy and me, I didn't feel her apology was adequate or sincere. She was too embarrassed herself to admit her mistake by apologizing in the same loud voice which she'd used for the accusations. She had caused quite a scene about the broken bell, and then she just dismissed it. Her weak apology seemed meaningless.

I replied, "Well, I should think you should be."

She turned around and gave me an icy stare. "I said I was sorry," she snapped. But saying the words is sometimes not enough. You have to mean what you say.

In marriage, family situations, and other relationships, the words "I'm sorry" are often hard to say. But when spoken from the heart, they can go a long way toward mending whatever is wrong.

✦ The Big Four-Oh

"Middle age" can be an ugly phrase. Translated, it means that once you've reached it, half of your life is over, the early parts of which you don't even remember. It's a gradual process: I remember watching a college basketball game when I was in my late twenties and suddenly realizing that the players were almost a decade younger than I was. In the last few years, I've realized that I'm even older than most pro athletes.

Several years ago, on the day before my fortieth birthday, someone doing a survey asked my age, and I replied, "Thirty-nine." Billy and David couldn't understand why I didn't say I'd be forty the next day. "When you're ten," I told the boys, "you'd probably be excited, and say 'I'll be eleven tomorrow,' but if you're thirty-nine, you just say thirty-nine." It was important for me to soak up every last day, hour and minute of being in my thirties.

Several years ago, I could feel the sobering wake-up call known as middle age looming just ahead. I knew I wanted to have another baby, our third child, but my husband wasn't so sure. I felt I was at a crossroads. There were roads I'd taken in life and others I decided not to follow. I felt a need to retrace my steps down a long-forgotten road. In college, I had taken a few drama courses and received positive comments from my professor and the other students, but I didn't pursue acting after that, choosing writing and raising a family instead. But as I approached this mid-life crossroads, I gathered my courage, memorized a monologue, and tried out for a local play. It was hard to fit this effort into my busy schedule with two sons, and I was pretty nervous about the audition. But it was something I simply *had* to do. My life would have been less stressful if I had chosen not to do it, but that wasn't an option.

When I arrived at the audition, the place was packed with about thirty other hopefuls. What in the world was I doing there? I had hoped I'd be one of the last ones to perform, but of course, I was randomly selected to go second. I got up there in front of everybody and began my monologue. The much-practiced lines came easily as my nervousness faded away. For an instant, I felt like I was really holding the audience in the palm of my hand, making them feel what my character was feeling. When they all burst into laughter at my funny last line, my spirit soared.

I didn't stick around to watch anyone else audition after my group was done. It didn't really matter to me whether or not I got a part in the play; the main thing was I had gotten up there and auditioned, revisiting a road that I thought I'd veered off a long time ago. The next day I found out I didn't get a part, but later that week I received a very nice handwritten note from the director, telling me how much she'd enjoyed my audition, that she couldn't see me in that particular play but that she hoped I'd audition again soon. (And that was okay with me because one of the questions we'd had to answer on the audition questionnaire was if we'd be willing to dye our hair green).

About two weeks after that, I found out I was pregnant with our third child, and my life has been a whirlwind ever since with three sons and numerous activities and responsibilities. I haven't been back to an audition. But that one night was all I needed. I had to prove something to myself.

I thought about that audition again as I approached the big four-oh. It is important that moms fulfill the other parts of who we are in order to be the best person we can be, which also makes us the best mother and wife we can be. If we ignore the pursuit of our hobbies and dreams, it is bound to have a detrimental effect.

That's why I still continue to write. I'll never forget the first time I went to a local writer's group after being at home with my first two sons for eight years and having no involvement in a creative circle. It was exhilarating to talk with people who shared my passion for expressing feelings and ideas with words, and I was on a natural high when I left. That's also why, after Jason's birth, I started teaching writing in schools part-time (well, that and Kevin said we could use the extra money). It made our lives even more hectic, but I didn't want to pass on the opportunity and then regret it later. My biggest dream in life has always been to have a family, but that doesn't mean I can't strive to make others dreams come true, too.

And we moms still have to do things for fun. I love to read, but it's rare I get the time to do so. I usually start novels while on vacation but am unable to finish them and end up forgetting about them; so I have about a dozen unfinished books gathering dust in various places about the house. Someday I'd like to find them all, put them in a pile, and read them from cover to cover, without misplacing a single one.

I also used to love to dance. Not ballet, or tap, or the waltz. But simply fast dance to upbeat pop music where you let your energy and your soul loose. A few months after Jason was born, I bought some CDs of eighties music, turned up the volume, and danced in our family room, bringing back the memories of my college days. My sons watched, bewildered. During a break in the music, David stared at me in disbelief and said slowly, "Mom, you're scaring me." It was like I was a stranger to them, but I wasn't a stranger—I was just being the old "me."

A fortieth birthday is a time to reflect on such things; its also a time to consider issues of vanity. Such as Botox treatments and spider vein injections. I began a close examination of myself as my fortieth approached. The vanity in me thought getting rid of wrinkles and ugly veins would be a great way to celebrate middle age. Yet, I couldn't afford to do both the Botox *and* the vein injections. Decisions, decisions. Hmmm. One morning while I was putting on my makeup under a florescent light, I noticed the wrinkle in the middle of my forehead again and thought, "Definitely the Botox." Then, while buying something at a sales counter in the mall, I caught a glimpse of the back of my legs in a mirror behind me. "Ugh," I said to myself. "Definitely the veins."

As it turned out, we decided to get our kitchen cabinets redone instead. No Botox, no vein injections. The practical side of me won out. Should I choose to wow my friends and old boyfriends with smooth, clear skin or get a built-in spice rack instead? No contest.

For my fortieth birthday, Kevin very sweetly arranged and paid for a "girls only" birthday dinner for me, my mother, two sisters, and some good friends of mine at one of my favorite restaurants. Afterward, my friends and I went to a nightclub to celebrate my fortieth. As we sat there trying to adjust ourselves to the smoke-filled room, we put our pocketbooks on a ledge in front of us. I looked at all four purses lined up there in a row. Mine looked like the equivalent of a roller derby queen among ballerinas. It was big. It was ugly. And it was *practical.* I leaned over to my friends, pointed to my handbag, and shouted above the music, "That *looks* like the purse of a forty-year-old woman, doesn't it?" They all laughed and readily agreed.

So the next morning I went to the mall to buy a new purse. But as I paid for it, I tried to avoid glimpsing the back of my legs in that mirror again. The spider vein fund is all used up on—how exciting—new cabinetry. Well, hopefully on my fiftieth the roof won't need to be reshingled and Jason won't need braces, so I can finally spend some money on me.

◆ Lessons Jacob Taught

No graduation ceremonies are ordinary. Each one represents years of individual struggles and accomplishments, laughter and tears, disappointments and dreams. But when my twenty-one-year-old nephew, Jacob, graduated from college in the spring of 2006, it was particularly emotional to see him walk across that stage to receive his diploma. Few people have had to overcome as much as he has endured in his young life.

Graduations symbolically represent one's growing up and stepping into adulthood, ready to take on the world. Yet Jacob left his childhood behind him much earlier than most. He was diagnosed with an aggressive leukemia when he was almost nine—the spring of 1993. Faced with his own mortality and the death of friends he'd met at the hospital, Jacob was forced to grow up quickly. It seems like eons ago in some ways, and still, in others, it seems like yesterday.

On the night of the diagnosis, Kevin and I had been watching the UNC-Michigan NCAA championship basketball game on TV. We'd just gotten Billy down for the night, and I was halfheartedly watching the game, more focused on the fact that Jacob's pediatrician had sent him to the hospital because his blood cell count was unbalanced. We weren't sure what to expect; we hoped for a diagnosis like low iron, but we were bracing for worse news like diabetes. The possibility of cancer was something we'd thought about, but didn't consider as very probable.

The phone call came while we were watching the game. I couldn't bring myself to answer at first, so Kevin grabbed it. "She's right here," he mumbled, holding the phone out to me with a look on his face I'd never seen before. I knew it was my mother.

"Hey," I said.

"They say it's definitely leukemia," my mother told me, her voice cracking.

"Oh God, Mama, no," I moaned. "Not leukemia." Kevin leaned back hard against the wall and slid down into a crouching position, covering his face with his hands.

I asked about my sister Gail and her husband—Jacob's parents. "They're devastated," Mama said. Suddenly, I couldn't breathe, as if I were literally suffocating. I needed air. I handed the phone to Kevin and ran out into the yard, where rain was steadily streaming down. I screamed, and then I cried as I paced wildly back and forth, oblivious to the rain. As I sat there getting drenched, I realized I had used the word "devastated" much too casually over the years. I remembered saying things like, "I'm devastated I didn't get that job," or even "I'm devastated my team didn't win the big game." That hadn't been devastation at all. That night, I learned what the word truly means, the way it feels; I vowed never to use it in casual terms again.

The emotions of that time are still raw, still on the surface, and all it takes to bring the tears again is a moment of reliving those awful days and nights. The overwhelming diagnosis; the chemo; the search for a matching bone marrow donor; the thrill of finally finding one in the Netherlands; the wait to see if the transplant was successful; and of course, the relief and joy when we realized it was.

It's been a long road for Jacob, and for my sister, her husband, and Jacob's two brothers, Sam and Matthew. There were many setbacks and obstacles. But Jacob has never looked back and asked "why me?" or complained about the bumps or obstacles along the way. Now, there are other roads awaiting him, byways that will show him the good things in life. I know he'll choose the right roads, the right direction, as he's done before. He's learned the hard way what's important in life, and in the process he has made others aware of these gifts and inspired a new perspective on life within all of us so close to him.

Jacob has done very well in school, has won awards, and was consistently on the Dean's list. He's especially known for his computer expertise, and he even created my website, momsofboys.org. Although graduation is a time to reflect on what one has derived from the college experience, I found myself thinking more about what Jacob has taught, rather than what he's learned.

When Jacob was about five or six, he played in a basketball league that was very competitive, despite the young ages. Parents would cheer on their budding Michael Jordans from the sidelines, yelling unsolicited advice about dribbling and shooting. Jacob always seemed unaware of all that; he was more content to focus on family members and friends, who were there to watch him play. He waved often while he was on the court, prompting lots of smiles. He always knew family was important. I don't remember who won any of those games, but I do remember sitting in the stands waving and being so proud that Jacob was my nephew.

Whenever I become worried about trivial things and need to put life back in perspective, all I have to do is remember a story my sister, Jacob's mom, told me years ago. She and Jacob were in their car one morning when Jacob was in the middle of his chemotherapy and waiting to find a marrow donor—

his only chance of survival. Driving down the road, my sister felt overwhelmed by her profound grief, as though the world weighed on her shoulders. Then the silence of the car was broken as Jacob started happily singing, *"Zip a dee doo dah, zip a dee ay; My oh my what a wonderful day..."* My sister said a lump rose in her throat as she thought of what he was going through, and yet he could still sing as if he didn't have a care in the world. Lessons like that are simply not taught in the classroom.

During the time of Jacob's transplant and recovery, I was pregnant with David. The mental image I envisioned through that pregnancy was a healthy, post-transplant Jacob holding my healthy newborn baby—his cousin—in his arms. I decided that picture in my mind would be my focal point to concentrate on while I was in labor. Ironically, I went into labor during Jacob's tenth birthday party. At the hospital when I did the breathing exercises, I imagined that every time I breathed out I was blowing all of Jacob's cancer cells out of him for good. It was the easiest labor of my three childbirths. Later, I was thrilled to see my mental image become a reality: a healthy Jacob holding David, my newborn.

Years later we went to a go-cart track to celebrate David's eighth birthday. David was too young to drive on the big track by himself, so he rode a two-seater with eighteen-year-old Jacob behind the wheel. As they sped off down the track together, I thought of that mental picture I had years earlier of the two of them together. Tears burned my eyes. I watched as Jacob maneuvered the go-cart safely through traffic, steering self-assuredly and strong. Then he accelerated and zoomed away again, around a curve, down another road. Out of sight.

Catch him if you can.

✦ As Time Goes By

I FELT THE pang in my heart when I drove into the carpool lane to pick up David on his first day of sixth grade in middle school. My eyes searched the courtyard area, where students gathered to wait for their rides. Automatically, I looked for his older brother towering over the crowd as I had been doing the past three years, but then I remembered my older son was now in high school. I was here to pick up son No. 2.

That's when the feeling hit me, intense and all-encompassing, filling every crevice of my being. How do we go through time not realizing how quickly it passes until so much of it is gone? It seemed strange that my oldest, Billy, was no longer a student there, instead replaced by his younger brother, who was ready to forge ahead into the perils of middle school. It was like the changing of the guard. Through watery eyes, I looked again toward the group of students.

And then I saw him. My heart jumped. There David sat on a bench looking at the sidewalk, lost in thought, with his newly acquired trombone in hand, lunchbox resting on his knee, backpack hanging to one side. He still looked like my little boy to me, yet he was on the verge of adolescence. Suddenly, I pictured him as an infant, during those days when he first learned to roll over, lying on the family room floor, a blanket draped over his head as he grinned up at me. And this image stirred another pang inside me.

Emotions run high when a new school year begins—a time of changes and new challenges. I had known it was coming. There were even some precursors, previous events here and there that signaled what was ahead.

When David was ten, he "bridged over" from Cub Scouts to Boy Scouts, signifying an important milestone in his life. Every year at the Blue & Gold Banquet, Cub Scouts are recognized for their achievements, and the oldest Cubs become Boy Scouts in a highly anticipated symbolic ceremony. As each boy stands on stage, his parents take off his Cub Scout hat and necker-chief (some moms try to give them a quick kiss, but others have been told not to by their sons). Then he shakes hands with his leaders and turns to walk across an actual wooden bridge to meet his new Boy Scout leaders on the other side, who present him with a new cap and neckerchief. It's always a meaningful ceremony that causes some tears and sniffles, especially when it's your own son up there. I've been through it with both Billy and David, and it is definitely a moment to remember. Scout-ing is a wonderful program that helps the boys to understand the importance of setting and attaining goals, while becoming more independent.

The bridging event takes place at the banquet—the Blue & Gold dinner—where awards are presented and speeches are given. It usually lasts a few hours. I was attending one such Blue & Gold ceremony when I was pregnant with Jason. I had recently found out that we'd be having yet another boy, so when I came in, other Scout moms turned and smiled, and some asked, "Just how many more of these ceremonies will you have to sit through?" Of course, they were referring to all the years of Scouts awaiting my third boy.

Life is indeed about crossing bridges.

When Jason was about a year old, he was playing on the floor one night, wrestling with his brothers. He was grinning from ear to ear, his blonde hair tousled. Billy, then ten, sat up and gazed at Jason, a look of pure love on his face. He turned to me and said wistfully, "I'm going to miss him when he's not a baby anymore, you know?"

I stared at Billy, my first-born, who was so tall, even at ten, that he wore a size sixteen shoe. "Yeah, Billy," I whispered, smiling. "I know."

Then they went on with wrestling, but I felt tears come to my eyes. I knew exactly what Billy was talking about because I'd sometimes think about my older sons and things they had said or done when they were toddlers, trying to recall the feel of their hand in mine or the sound of their uncontrollable squeals and laughter as I chased them around the kitchen.

I mentioned what Billy said to my mother a few days later, as the two of us sat in my parents' living room, surrounded by photos of my three siblings and me and all of our families. When I told her Billy said he'd miss his baby brother as Jason got older, she smiled knowingly and said, "Oh, I still miss all of y'all like that." I heard the emotion in her voice and choked back my own feelings as I gave her a quick hug. I thought of the old photo albums and all the eight millimeter films that my father had taken as we'd grown up. Somehow I suddenly missed those kids, too.

I'm the first to admit I can be overly emotional about how quickly time passes. I once popped in a new Barney tape for Jason, this one a ten-year reunion of the past kids on the show. I used to watch Barney with Billy when the program first became popular. There was one kid on the show named Michael, a blonde who was sort of the ringleader of the children. So when he was introduced on the reunion tape as a teenager with a deep voice, my eyes welled with tears as I realized how much time had passed. I pointed to Michael and asked Billy, "Remember him?"

Billy looked over at the TV. "Mom," he said, "he's like seventeen and still dancing to 'I'm a Little Teapot.'" He rolled his eyes, evidently not touched by the passage of time as I was.

There was also the time Kevin and I were driving back from a relative's wedding, and I began sniffling. "What's the matter with you?" Kevin asked.

"Nothing," I replied. I looked out of the passenger window, again becoming teary.

"What is it?" he repeated.

"I'm just thinking about Billy's wedding."

Kevin narrowed his eyes and looked over at me. "He's twelve, Sharon," he said.

Some day my boys will be men. That's both exciting and scary, just as it's probably always been for moms of boys. I hope and pray each of them becomes a good person, a man of faith, a wonderful husband and father. A happy person who enjoys lots of success. A man who is loved unconditionally. I look forward to seeing them grow and become those men.

Yet, I also fear the future. I think about the threat of war and what that might mean for my sons. This threat used to seem so far away, but as Billy enters his mid-teens, I realize the possibility of his being drawn into war as something very real and close. Sometimes I imagine my sons dressed in soldiers' uniforms, their blue eyes peering from under their helmets. I have to shake my head to make this vision go away. My heart goes out to the parents whose children are serving their country in this way.

There are times when I've watched my sons sleeping and

wished all the world could watch a sleeping child, and then surely there would be no more wars. They are so peaceful and so beautiful when they're asleep. At the age of three, Jason started sleeping each night with a stuffed white bear he named, "Soft Friend." To see him with his arms wrapped tightly around the bear was truly a moving experience. Watching my sons sleep brings out my protective instincts. During these times I remember, despite their rough and tough exteriors, boys are still children who need their moms.

We're here to answer those never-ending questions from preschoolers like, "Why did God make lightning, Mommy?" "Do trees get sleepy?" "Why do people make bad choices?" "What's going to happen when I grow up? Can I still live here with you and Dad?"

Jason, like all boys, does indeed have a sensitive side to him. One night when he was four, we were about to say our bedtime prayers, when he asked me, "Are you going to get old, Mom?" I explained to him that everybody gets older, that life would be boring if we stayed the same. He reached out to hug me, sobbing, "I don't want you to get old!" His feelings touched me deeply that night and made me realize that our boys have a lot going on in their minds and souls. Even Twerp.

Jason has asked me such questions in the past as he was trying to figure out the world, which is pretty much what my older boys are doing in their own way. Moms are here to worry about things, too. Even when Billy was a year and a half away from getting his driver's license, I'd take notes about things to tell him to watch for at certain intersections in town. Overboard? No, it was just being a mom.

And despite the sibling rivalry and countless arguments

between brothers, they take up for each other when the situation calls for it. When David was three, I remember some pushy kids on the playground making fun of his unclear speech. Before I could rush to his defense, six-year-old Billy was there, pushing himself in between the kids and his brother, right up in their faces. "You don't say that stuff to my brother," he said in as menacing of a voice as a six-year-old could muster. My heart swelled as I witnessed the love and protectiveness Billy showed for his brother.

They take pride in one another and their accomplishments. Whenever David had a great outing on the pitching mound, I'd see a smile tug at Billy's lips as he watched. When Billy made a great play in a basketball game, David would say things like, "Did you see that block?" Or when the older boys would watch Jason play soccer, they'd clap and cheer his every move—even when he got down on the field and started doing push-ups after a goal. Sure, maybe Jason would throw toy fire trucks at them occasionally, but it was plain to see Billy and David adored their "baby" brother. And Jason would run to meet his brothers when they'd go to the water fountain during their games. He'd pat them on the back and say, "You're doing great out there."

As they grow older, they will appreciate all the memories they have of growing up. Yes, our house is loud, and laundry will one day be spilling out the windows. But this is what being a boy is all about. They do define my identity—I'm their mom first and foremost—and that's fine. Many people say that when boys grow up, they aren't as close to their moms as girls are. The possibility of that makes my heart ache. I don't want to lose their affection. One of my favorite quotes comes from

Gabriel Garcia Marquez, who wrote, "She discovered with great delight that one does not love one's children just because they are one's children but because of the friendship formed while raising them." And I certainly feel that with my sons as they get older. I hope they always know that I love them unconditionally and consider the time I spent raising them the best years of my life, from that first cry in the hospital to their first awkward steps to those first dates.

When Billy started kindergarten, he was really eager and ready for it to finally arrive. I was looking forward to being able to spend some time alone with David as I'd had with Billy. So when I took Billy in that first morning and saw the PTA had organized a "Tissue Tea" for teary-eyed kindergarten moms, I thought, "Tissues? Heck, where's the confetti?" Yet as Jason neared his first day of kindergarten, I completely understood the need for a tissue tea. It is hard to let go sometimes, to move on to another chapter of our lives—for both me and my sons.

A few years ago when Billy's voice changed, becoming deeper than I'd ever imagined, I was watching a videotape of Billy and David holding Jason after he was first born. Suddenly, I heard this childish, high-pitched voice say something, and I was astonished that the words were coming out of Billy's mouth, who was nine then. "Oh, my gosh," I exclaimed to Kevin, "that's Billy talking! Listen to his voice." Emotions flushed through me as I watched my little boy and listened to a voice I'd never hear again except on recordings. It was a strange feeling indeed. A good friend of mine hasn't changed her message on her answering machine in three years because her son recorded it before his voice changed, and she can't bring herself to erase it. It's easy for a mom to get emotional about the passage of time and the physical changes that signify the process of maturity, from the deepening voice to those first few scraggly facial hairs.

The day I first noticed Billy was taller than I was really made me feel odd. I was looking up—literally—to my "little boy." I asked Billy soon afterward if looking down at me made him feel strange. He grinned, and to my surprise said, "Yeah, it sort of does." I was glad this had affected him also and that I wasn't alone in my wonder of this change. It unnerved six-foot-three Kevin when Billy grew even taller than he is. "But I've still got you by thirty pounds," Kevin told him. Now, David is almost my height. It doesn't seem possible.

Lots of parenthood moments are bittersweet, evoking the need for both confetti and tissues. As our sons become men, it is amazing to watch them grow and change on this journey, forming their values and building their character along the way. Despite the teasing I give my husband, I would be overjoyed if they became men as good and honorable as he is (though they could learn to listen a bit better than their dad).

I'm sure there will always be moments when I lament never having a daughter. I once saw my twenty-five-year-old niece, Kristin, sitting in my mother's kitchen, talking about something that had happened at work, and I noticed that my sister, Mary, Kristin's mom, draped her arm casually over Kristin's arm—a sign of their close relationship. For an instant, I ached for the daughter I would never have. Even though I hope and expect to have continued close relationships with my sons, I knew it wouldn't be quite like what Kristin and Mary have. Kristin recently got married, and I can't quite describe what I felt when I first saw her in her wedding dress: a bittersweet mixture of pride, joy, and emptiness. Of course, someday I will probably be the mother of a groom, and though it doesn't have the traditional connotation that "mother of the bride" does, it is a day I look forward to, a day I will treasure being the "mom of boys."

Mothers are keenly aware of the precious passage of time and what it means as our sons get older. "Hold my hand, Billy," I used to say as we crossed a parking lot or street. I can still remember the feel of his small, soft hand in mine, how our fingers entwined, how I wanted to keep him safe forever. Memories like this stay fixed in our minds. We envision their young, dirt-streaked faces even as we gaze proudly at our grownup sons on their wedding day.

Of course, we moms of boys need to make sure we get in good with the daughters-in-law, too, and that we do things to make them like us. I hope to bypass the stereotypes and become a much-loved mother-in-law. I'm already planning on giving my boys' wives gift certificates to great restaurants. Maybe movie passes, too. And I'll have lots of neat toys at my house, so the grandkids will want to come to see me. And I'll acknowledge to her that, yes, my son's a guy, and as such, sometimes he can be a real pain. I figure it's never too early to start planning my strategy.

My boys share a bond called "brotherhood," and although they might not realize it now, that's their father's and my gift to them to carry with them through the years, even long after we're gone. My prayer is that they remember fondly their years growing up and cherish their bond always as they cross the many bridges of life.

✦ ✦ ✦

Acknowledgments

AFTER TEASING AND picking on him as much as I do in this book, I'd better thank my husband, Kevin, before anyone else. Thanks, honey, for being supportive of me and my dream to someday have a book published. I'd also, of course, like to thank my three sons, Billy, David, and Jason, for allowing me (well, actually they didn't have much choice in the matter) to let others peek inside our lives. (Please don't sue me later, okay?) We are always busy, and life is hectic, but in the end, my boys make it all worthwhile with their hugs and their laughter. I'm proud to be their mom. Thanks to my whole family for putting up with me when I'd stay up until three in the morning writing, making me tired and irritable the next day.

I'd also like to thank my parents, Sam and Wiloree Johnson, who have always been there for me with their love and encouragement. God has blessed me to have them as my Mama and Daddy, and I would not be the person I am today without them and the wonderful childhood they helped build for me and the opportunities they gave me. My older brother, Sam, and two sisters, Gail and Mary, have also been marvelous throughout the years, and I'm glad we're friends as well as siblings. I treasure the memories that we have together as a family.

To my nieces, Kristin, Melissa, and Victoria—please

remember that you are amazing young women with so much to offer to this world and to others. You are in a sense the "daughters" I never had. (If my boys don't come to see me in the rest home, please, will you?) And to my nephews, Justin, Jacob, Sam, and Matthew, I had you guys in my life before my own sons, and I cherish those times with you. You are each extraordinary, talented young men. To my large extended family of aunts, uncles, cousins, and in-laws, it is a special feeling to know I am part of the lives of each one of you. I appreciate your interest in all that I've done and thank you for your prayers. And this book is also dedicated to the memory of those loved ones we've lost along the way who taught us what it means to be a family—particularly both sets of my grandparents. Bless be the ties that bind.

I want to say thank you, also, to the congregation—past and present—of the close-knit church I grew up in, St. Barnabas Presbyterian in Raleigh. They gave me the foundation that everyone needs to grow. The members of First United Methodist of Cary have given me the nourishment and fellowship I need to continue that growth. I was also blessed to have the most inspiring teacher ever—my high school English teacher, the late Muriel Allison.

A heartfelt thanks also to all my friends, who have tolerated me and listened to me vent from time to time about living with all guys and who've provided me with much-needed girls' nights out. Robyn, Michelle, Amy, and Tina have been special people whom God placed in my path of life. Thanks to my sister-in-law, Joan, who read my first draft of this book and gave me her feedback. To my mother-in-law, thanks for being a good sport about the two very tongue-in-cheek mother-in-law jokes in the book (please don't cut us out of the will). And thanks to the members of the local Moms of Boys group in the Raleigh/ Cary area, who have also been instrumental in my pursuing publication of this book, as well as to all those moms I've met through my website, www.momsofboys.org.

The writers' group I've been lucky enough to belong to for the past ten years has been a profound blessing in my life, providing not only valuable feedback and advice but also friendship. Our first group leader, Brenda Smart, died of cancer several years ago; she was the person who encouraged me to come to that first meeting. I will always remember her and the dedication she had to writing. And to our current leader, Bren Witchger, I greatly appreciate your suggestions and all your help. To former *Cary News* editor, Jane Paige, and current editor, Keith King, I appreciate the opportunity you gave me to write a regular column.

Thanks so much to the terrific people at Jefferson Press— Henry, Charlotte, and David—who could relate to the "raising boys" humor in my writing and wanted to publish my essays. Thanks also to my agent, Rob Wilson, who believed in my book enough to take me on as a client.

And thank you, God, for giving me the strength and patience not to give up the pursuit of my dreams.